W9-BYA-510

Your Complete Guide to Making Millions with Your Simple Idea or Invention

Insider Secrets You Need to Know

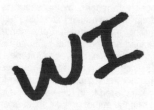

JANESSA CASTLE

YOUR COMPLETE GUIDE TO MAKING MILLIONS WITH YOUR SIMPLE IDEA OR INVENTION: INSIDER SECRETS YOU NEED TO KNOW

Copyright © 2011 by Atlantic Publishing Group, Inc.
1405 SW 6th Ave. • Ocala, Florida 34471 • 800-814-1132 • 352-622-1875–Fax
Website: www.atlantic-pub.com • E-mail: sales@atlantic-pub.com
SAN Number: 268-1250

Library of Congress Cataloging-in-Publication Data

Castle, Janessa, 1981–
  Your complete guide to making millions with your simple idea or invention: Insider secrets you need to know / by Janessa Castle.
      p. cm.
  Includes bibliographical references.
  ISBN-13: 978-1-60138-145-3 (alk. paper)
  ISBN-10: 1-60138-145-X (alk. paper)
  1. Inventions. 2. Patents. I. Title.
  T212.C38 2010
  608.773--dc22

                                        2010038432

PROJECT MANAGER: Shannon McCarthy
BOOK PRODUCTION DESIGN: T.L. Price • design@tlpricefreelance.com
PROOFREADER: Gretchen Pressley • phygem@gmail.com
COVER DESIGNS: Jackie Miller • millerjackiej@gmail.com

Printed on Recycled Paper

Printed in the United States

We recently lost our beloved pet "Bear," who was not only our best and dearest friend but also the "Vice President of Sunshine" here at Atlantic Publishing. He did not receive a salary but worked tirelessly 24 hours a day to please his parents.

Bear was a rescue dog that turned around and showered myself, my wife, Sherri, his grandparents Jean, Bob, and Nancy, and every person and animal he met (maybe not rabbits) with friendship and love. He made a lot of people smile every day.

We wanted you to know that a portion of the profits of this book will be donated to The Humane Society of the United States. *—Douglas & Sherri Brown*

The human-animal bond is as old as human history. We cherish our animal companions for their unconditional affection and acceptance. We feel a thrill when we glimpse wild creatures in their natural habitat or in our own backyard.

Unfortunately, the human-animal bond has at times been weakened. Humans have exploited some animal species to the point of extinction.

The Humane Society of the United States makes a difference in the lives of animals here at home and worldwide. The HSUS is dedicated to creating a world where our relationship with animals is guided by compassion. We seek a truly humane society in which animals are respected for their intrinsic value, and where the human-animal bond is strong.

Want to help animals? We have plenty of suggestions. Adopt a pet from a local shelter, join The Humane Society and be a part of our work to help companion animals and wildlife. You will be funding our educational, legislative, investigative, and outreach projects in the U.S. and across the globe.

Or perhaps you'd like to make a memorial donation in honor of a pet, friend, or relative? You can through our Kindred Spirits program. And if you'd like to contribute in a more structured way, our Planned Giving Office has suggestions about estate planning, annuities, and even gifts of stock that avoid capital gains taxes.

Maybe you have land you would like to preserve as a lasting habitat for wildlife. Our Wildlife Land Trust can help you. Perhaps the land you want to share is a backyard — that's enough. Our Urban Wildlife Sanctuary Program will show you how to create a habitat for your wild neighbors.

So you see, it's easy to help animals. And The HSUS is here to help.

THE HUMANE SOCIETY
OF THE UNITED STATES

2100 L Street NW • Washington, DC 20037 • 202-452-1100
www.hsus.org

Dedication

This book is dedicated to the most important people in my life.

To my husband Matt, daughter Madison, and son Braden for all of their love, encouragement, and understanding.

To my parents, Janet and Dave, for their unending support and for always making me believe that I can do anything.

Table of Contents

Chapter 2:
Researching Your Idea   41

Chapter 3:
Protecting Your Idea   61

Chapter 4:
Patents   69

Chapter 5:
Other Intellectual Property
Protections · 105

Chapter 6:
Designing Your Idea · · · · · · · · · · · · · · · · · 121

Chapter 7:
Transforming the Design
into a Product   131

Chapter 8:
Selling or Licensing Your Idea   143

Chapter 9:
Commercialization on Your Own   159

Chapter 10:
Manufacturing Your Product   177

Chapter 11:
Traditional Marketing   187

Chapter 12:
Marketing via the Internet   211

Chapter 13:
Beware of Scam Artists   231

Appendix   241

Foreword

For more than ten years, I have been writing articles and commentaries in the hope of educating independent inventors and small businesses on patent and intellectual property issues. For those new to the innovation business, it can be an extremely daunting task to get up to speed on the topic, particularly given the diverse, sometimes counterintuitive, issues and obstacles that need to be successfully navigated. I have long wanted to write a book for inventors myself, but now there is no need for that endeavor. Simply stated, if I were to write a book on the topic, it would have been this book. Repeatedly, as I read this book, I found myself nodding my head in complete agreement. For new inventors who seriously want to succeed, *Your Complete Guide to Making Millions with Your Simple Idea or Invention* should be required reading.

As the U.S. economy continues to trend toward innovation and technology, intellectual property rights, and patent rights in particular, have continued to become more important. To paraphrase Bruce Springsteen: The manufacturing jobs are gone, and they are not coming back, as many

Americans well know. Prosperity is tied to innovation, and a prerequisite to successfully innovating and making money from innovation is to understand the process, which is capably and thoroughly set forth by the author, Janessa Castle.

I am constantly preaching to inventors that they are far more likely to succeed if they treat inventing as a business. Yes, inventing can be fun, and for many, there are great rewards in figuring out useful solutions to problems. For most, they look at inventing as a way to participate in the American dream. The inventors I encounter every day want to be recognized for their innovative contributions, but they also would like to succeed financially. There is absolutely nothing wrong with that.

The overarching theme of this book is to approach inventing in a business-responsible way. Many who are unfamiliar with the trials and tribulations of inventors frequently fail to realize that inventors are highly intelligent and creative, but as with all intelligent and creative individuals engaged in a project, they need direction. Castle guides inventors in gentle but firm ways, explaining what might otherwise seem obvious. But when you work with inventors daily, you realize they might not always be business-savvy. So, when Castle starts by explaining the importance of time management, scheduling, and meeting promised deadlines, she demonstrates an uncommon level of understanding with respect to the questions inventors have and the knowledge they absolutely need to succeed.

There are many books for inventors and would-be entrepreneurs, and almost universally when I read them, I find myself thinking about what is missing and what should be included. Not with this book. Other books that are not lacking are instead overwhelming. This book addresses every issue of real consequence in a way that is thorough but still approachable. In reading this book, novices will learn the issues that deserve attention, and

I would wager that even experienced inventors would find inspiration and learn valuable lessons. The marketing tips and suggestions are sound, not pie-in-the-sky. Actionable intelligence is provided on topic after topic, even down to issues almost universally overlooked, such as product packaging. If you want to sell it, the package needs to be attractive and garner the appropriate attention without being over the top, and most importantly, it needs to be stackable and fit on the shelf.

So much of what is contained within these pages addresses the common questions of inventors. It also raises issues you likely would not have thought of on your own that need to be understood and appreciated. I wholeheartedly recommend this book and will be suggesting to my clients that if they are serious about succeeding with their inventions, they absolutely need to read it. Not everyone will make millions on his or her inventions, but armed with this information, it will be far more likely.

*Gene Quinn is a U.S. patent attorney, law professor, and the founder of IPWatchdog.com. He is a principal lecturer in the top patent bar review course in the nation, which helps aspiring patent attorneys and patent agents prepare themselves to pass the patent bar exam. Quinn is also the inventor of a unique invention mining and patent drafting system, known as the Invent + Patent System, which enables the submission of detailed answers that form the basis of an extraordinarily detailed invention disclosure. It can be filed immediately as a provisional patent application or subsequently reviewed, modified, edited, and supplemented by a patent attorney or agent before being filed as a nonprovisional patent application. Quinn started the popular intellectual property website **http://ipwatchdog.com** in 1999, and since that time, the site has had millions of unique visitors.*

Introduction

From calendars and plywood to staplers and contact lenses, inventions are an important source of convenience in modern life. The creativity, motivation, and insightfulness of inventors have made everyday tasks much simpler.

A look at an ordinary morning illustrates how important inventions are during our daily routine. Many of us begin the day by waking up to an alarm clock, a handy gadget that has added much convenience — and sometimes frustration — to our lives. After hitting the snooze button, you get out of bed and head to the bathroom. There, the toilet and indoor plumbing mean you do not have to go outside to answer nature's call. Already, you may be thankful for the modern bathroom's conveniences, and we have not even gotten to soap, deodorant, shampoo, toothpaste, and toilet paper. After getting dressed, you head to the kitchen for breakfast. The refrigerator offers you the convenience of fresh food saved from spoiling, and the coffee maker gurgles as it prepares its brew. After breakfast, you grab your cell phone or laptop before getting in your car and heading to work.

All of these products started out as ideas and have become staples in our lives because their inventors took the necessary steps to turn those ideas into reality. It might seem as though we need nothing else to make our lives better or more convenient, but new inventions hit the market every year. Some come from an idea for something entirely new. Others improve upon a product that already exists. Parents used to boil a pot of water and submerge their baby bottles into the water to warm it. An inventor noticed a need for an electric bottle-warming device — plug it in, sometimes add a little water, turn it on, and wait for the bottle to warm. After this became possible, a need was observed for on-the-go bottle warming. Instead of mothers using the hot water from sinks in public restrooms to warm a bottle, a battery-operated bottle warmer was invented, which saved mothers plenty of time and frustration. Now, there are bottle warmers that plug into the lighter socket in a car. With each invention, the ease and convenience of bottle warming has improved. Ideas for inventions can come from new technology, but they can also come from making an already successful product more convenient or easier to use.

If you are an imaginative person with a good idea and the desire to get that idea out into the world, this book is for you. An idea for an invention brings you no money or fame until it is out of your brain and into the hands of consumers. This book will guide you through the process of getting your idea to the marketplace in the fastest possible time and most cost-effective way. By the time you finish reading, your invention will be on its way to the consumer market.

About This Book

The invention process is a long, complex road. *How to Turn Your Simple Idea or Invention into Millions: Insider Secrets You Need to Know* will explain the steps you need to take to transform your invention from an idea in your head to a product on store shelves. It will lead you through a course of action any inventor can follow to develop a successful, coordinated product. This book will guide you through the most important stage of starting a new business: having a clever, original idea and transforming it into a successful product. *For information about the different types of businesses, see the Appendix.*

If you have ever seen a commercial for a product and thought to yourself, "Hey, I thought of that years ago," remember that even though you may have considered the product idea, someone else is raking in the profits. Thinking up an invention does not make you any money. You must take that idea through several steps from research and manufacturing to marketing and distribution. You will learn in this book about every step of the invention process. This book is your guide to converting your creative idea into a product consumers are snatching off the shelves.

CHAPTER 1:

The Invention Process

"America demands invention
and innovation to succeed."

— KIT BOND, U.S. SENATOR AND
FORMER MISSOURI GOVERNOR

For some inventors, coming up with the idea is the easy part. Bringing that idea to market may be more difficult. Before you can transform your idea into a product for consumers to buy, you must conduct market research and develop a strategy that blends protection of your ideas with commercialization. Every successful invention has answered a consumer need by providing some type of benefit or service, and they all began with one thing: a good idea. This book will take you through the steps of turning your idea into a money-making machine. Making millions from your idea can be a reality if you are equipped with the knowledge of how to get it done.

When you think of great inventors, Leonardo Da Vinci, the famous Italian artist and inventor, Alexander Graham Bell, the inventor of the telephone, or Thomas Edison, the mastermind behind the light bulb and the phonograph, might be some of the first who come to mind. However, not all inventors can be so renown. The world has seen numerous inventors who never made the history books but who have greatly affected our daily lives. For example, almost every home and office will have ballpoint pens rattling around in pen holders, but most people do not know László Bíró from Hungary invented them. Even something as simple and unremarkable (nowadays) as paper still came directly from the mind of an inventor. The ancient Egyptians used a form of paper called papyrus, but at the beginning of the second century in China, Cai Lun improved the manufacturing technology and invented the type of paper used today. You may take these convenient, everyday items for granted, but at one time they did not exist. Inventors created these products either out of a basic need or a desire to better their surroundings.

Every invention started as a just creative idea or vision, and every person has the ability to create such a gadget. Consider a routine or habitual problem in life — maybe you have an idea that could fix or at least lessen this unwanted situation. Perhaps you dreamed up a practical invention that makes some aspect of life more convenient, thought of an idea for a new piece of technology, or contemplated a way to improve upon a current product. You might have just brushed this idle thought to the back of your mind, only to later see on the news that someone made millions off the same idea. But it doesn't have to be this way. It is entirely possible to create an invention from an idea, market it for yourself, and use that product as the main source of income for your business. The next newly famous person making millions could be you.

You have the idea for your invention — it might be a basic concept, or it might be pretty well developed. Regardless, your first step is to look at your idea from different angles because there is always room for more research and exploration. Your invention has to impress people enough to make them think they cannot live without it.

Some Aspects of Inventing

The invention process can be rewarding, but several factors can cause major headaches. Take a moment to consider the following aspects before diving in.

Time management

Potential inventors have to learn the importance of time management. When you are involved in any creative project, one of the worst things you can be is oblivious of time. If you wait for inspiration to strike or if you put off working until the right creative mood hits, you will end up achieving nothing. In order to move forward in the process, you need to use your time efficiently by constantly having material to work with and improve upon.

When starting a creative project, make sure you will be able to complete it in a reasonable amount of time. Construct a timetable for your project, and set realistic targets. Always build in a bit of contingency time for things to go wrong. If you work alone, you will need to be your own project manager. This calls for vast amounts of self-discipline. Setting a schedule can help you manage your time. If you are working for yourself, set aside certain hours each week — or each day — to devote to your invention. Make a list of things you want to accomplish during each work session, and manage your time to achieve these goals. It is important to commit yourself entirely to achieving individual tasks. In the beginning, you might allot too much or too little time to certain tasks. As you get further along in the process, you will have a more reasonable idea of how long things will take, and you can adjust your schedule as needed.

You will quickly discover that buyers demand reliability. You may produce stunning, creative inventions, but if you do not meet your promised deadlines, you soon will find that clients stop purchasing from you. Managing your time properly will help you be a reliable inventor and improve your business.

Commitment

Commitment is essential to success. If you add a genuine and firm sense of commitment to your idea, research, and time-management skills, you are more likely to see your project through to its fruition. The invention process does not happen overnight. It may take years to get from an idea to a product to a sale. One way to remain committed to your invention is to remind yourself of the end result: your invention, a solution to an unfulfilled need and the stepping stone to your financial breakthrough. Because of the detailed process you must go through to get your invention to the commercial market, it can be difficult to remember the success waiting at the end. You will not reap any financial benefit until your project is in the hands of consumers, so keep reminding yourself that your utmost commitment at every stage will end in a payoff.

Perseverance

Creating, designing, and manufacturing an invention takes hard work. You will sometimes be frustrated and disappointed; you might even want to quit. Instead, step back to look at the larger picture, and remember you have a solid, authentic idea for a desirable invention. When your mind starts drifting toward these destructive thoughts, it is imperative to be confident in your idea and keep moving forward in the process.

Here are some tips to keep you going strong:

> **Make a plan:** Split the invention process up into several phases and create a time estimate for each one. Phases to include in your plan are research, development and design, patent search and application, manufacturing, and marketing and sales.

> **Stick with the plan:** In the beginning, you may find that your estimates are off the mark, but you will become more accurate with experience. If you veer off course, revise your plan.

> **Allow yourself breaks:** Take breaks at a time you have decided upon beforehand, and do not use a break as a distraction. When work is not flowing smoothly, it is easy to grab a snack, check an e-mail, or phone a friend for a chat. Problems are not solved that way; all you do is postpone finding a solution, and you lose valuable time.

> **Stay focused on the idea:** Most potential inventors are constantly looking for ways to improve life, and ideas may come to them on a weekly — if not daily — basis. Instead of bouncing from one idea to the next, remain focused on the project at hand.

Take an inventory of your skills

Many personal and professional skills will aid in the process of turning your idea into an invention. Inventors come from all backgrounds, but the skills discussed in coming chapters will help you understand which ones you already possess and which ones you may want to improve upon for your invention to be successful. The first thing you need to do is identify your strengths. Write down what you are good at. *To help you formulate your list, use the Appendix, which include a comprehensive checklist of skills that might help you when formulating your invention.* Once your create your list of strengths, go back and rate each skill from one to ten, one being the most favored, and ten being the least favored. At the end of this exercise, you will have identified at least two or three of your greatest strengths.

The Inventor and the Manufacturer Gap

Your prospective customers will not be considering your invention in a vacuum. They have a limited amount of capital and a variety of new products to consider purchasing. They will be choosing from competing inventions and product ideas when deciding where to put their resources.

Some inventors tend to innovate for the sake of innovation, and they run the risk of creating inventions that are irrelevant to the market. Technology should be used in the service of other goals. There must be a meshing of innovative technology from the inventor and usefulness or sales potential for the customer. If you want to tinker in your basement and come up with cool ideas to discuss with your innovative friends, then go for it. But if you want to make money from an invention, your new technology must have a purpose in today's market, not just exist for the sake of making new tehnology. Even if an invention is relevant to the end consumer, it may be irrelevant to the manufacturer, which has its own set of requirements. By focusing only on technological innovation and performance, inventors are likely to fall into one of several traps, which include:

> **Incredibly nifty inventions that cost a fortune to make:** If you are not considering the manufacturer's costs and capabilities, you are ignoring your own customer's needs.

> **The nuclear stapler:** This phrase describes creative technology that results in an over-engineered product or one that does not perform the task it is designed for. Just because you can do something does not mean you should. If you want to climb a mountain because it is there — go ahead. If you want to sell someone else on climbing it for that reason alone — good luck.

> **The hammer in search of a nail:** Technology in search of a problem is like a hammer in search of a nail. If there is no problem driving your solution, you have no built-in market for your product.

There are other reasons a company may not take an interest in your invention. These reasons might have nothing to do with the merits of your invention or your invention's fit with the company's market position. These could include:

> The not-invented-here syndrome arises, which means corporate executives or internal research and development staffs are hostile to outside ideas. Corporations that typically generate their own ideas are strongly aligned with a corporate culture, and companies that spend heavily on research and development could feel threatened by the possibility of outside influence.

> ➢ There is a lack of capital to pursue your product.

> ➢ A new direction or new product you are unaware of makes your invention obsolete.

You may never know why a company rejects your invention, but if you are convinced the invention is a good fit and has excellent potential, take it to another potential manufacturer or maybe even a competitor of the original company instead of losing heart.

Facts to Remember: From Patents to Sales

Whether you're creating only one product to sell to the public or forming an entire business around your idea, you need to know certain facts about idea creation. A **patent** is a grant issued by a governmental agency that bestows ownership rights of an idea to its inventor. Patents prevent others from making, selling, or using your invention without your permission. A number of patents have protected ideas that have a tremendous impact on many people's lives while helping the inventor make millions by keeping others from making the same invention. Some examples include the electric lamp, the transistor radio, and the auto engine.

Hundreds of products have failed in the market for various reasons. Even though a product got to the manufacturing stage, the inventor may not have taken the necessary steps to market or sell it. Marketing and sales are crucial to the success of your invention. Effective marketing promotes sales, which are crucial for investors.

Action Steps
....

This section will be at the end of each chapter and will provide an opportunity to assess your idea in different ways. Take this time and advice to help you evaluate your potential product. Experts agree that proper planning and examination of your idea will save you headaches down the road.

When evaluating your invention, several questions can help you decide whether a particular idea is genuinely important or only of passing interest:

1. **Is this a new idea?** Having an idea for a product already on the market will get you nowhere. Your idea must be a completely new product or an updated version of a product that already exists. *More information about determining if your idea is already on the market can be found in Chapter 2.*

2. **Is it a genuine improvement?** Some ideas may look good at first, but on closer inspection, they might be no better than what is already available. Mere novelty is not enough to qualify an idea as creative. If you have an idea for an invention that improves upon another product, it must be an improvement consumers will find valuable.

3. **Do the benefits outweigh the cost?** Any new idea or invention, however brilliant, will entail an element of cost. Your idea will catch on only if the cost of the product is in proportion with the benefit derived from it. For example, consumers would like a car that does not need gasoline to work but would not pay $200,000 for it because they would not be saving enough money in fuel costs.

4.   **Will it be capable of further improvement?** Some ideas are good because people can develop and improve on them over time. The invention of the computer is a good example. Thirty years ago, a computer was a large apparatus that needed its own air-conditioned room; only laboratories and large businesses could afford one. The computer has gotten smaller, faster, and cheaper so rapidly that it has become difficult to keep up with the rate of progress and advancing technology. The development of the computer stands as one of the best examples of creativity at work.

CASE STUDY: LESSONS FROM THE INVENTOR MENTOR

Jack Lander
Inventor Mentor
www.inventor-mentor.com

Jack Lander is a manufacturing engineer and product designer, inventor, and writer with books on financing inventions and a popular column in *Inventors Digest* magazine. He is a past president of the United Inventors Association, a nonprofit dedicated to helping inventors. He offers mentoring services for inventors for an hourly rate.

The first service any prospective client of Lander's receives is an evaluation of his or her invention's commercial potential. About 90 percent of inventions he receives have little commercial potential, so rather than continuing to work with these inventors, he sends them back to the drawing table. He does not tell them their inventions have no merit or that they would be fools to pursue it; rather, he points out weaknesses inventors can try to resolve.

For products with commercial potential, Lander helps clients define their concepts clearly, refine those concepts, and find inventor-friendly prototype makers. With his knowledge of manufacturing, Lander helps his clients decide what type of prototype they need so they are not wasting money on expensive molds or other production-oriented manufacturing investments at the prototype stage. He also shows his clients how to conduct market tests to ensure a market does exist for their invention. Next, he helps them decide what type of intellectual property to pursue, and then he directs his clients to prospective customers.

Lander recommends most of his clients initially pursue catalog companies, as they are inventor friendly.

"Chain stores predict their return on investment (ROI) on every square inch of shelf space," he said. "They do not want to gamble on products that lack a sales record because their calculation of ROI is based on market projections. Chain stores want product lines; they do not like to do business with companies selling a single product." Until you can show you have a reliable sales record and increasing sales, executives at these firms would be irresponsible to take on your product.

Catalog companies, on the other hand, "will deal with a company with a single product," Lander said. "They want innovative products that are not yet in stores because that is their niche. They do not request to inspect your facility either, so if you are operating out of your basement or garage, that's great because you are keeping the overhead low."

Lander also helps clients with design and marketing. In addition to his own design input, he refers clients to industrial designers if necessary and to prototype makers who also provide design input. If clients want a prototype that looks like the finished product, they will probably require industrial design assistance. If they want a prototype to prove the invention works or to test its functionality, a virtual prototype or a rough prototype that works but does not look just right will suffice.

"The reason they are prototype makers and not plain machinists is because they have that creativity in them; they want to participate in the design," he said.

Lander advocated saving money on design wherever possible and advertising the product to prospective licensees and distributors using what he calls a sell sheet, "a basic piece of paper to communicate to everyone," he said. "It gives them an idea of how to conceive of the invention." The sell sheet emphasizes the key benefits of a product and includes a photo or illustration and testimonials. Lander's clients use sell sheets to gauge interest in their product.

Although there are so many variables between resources, goals, inventions, and industries, a general outline of the process is possible. Lander charges $295 for his report, which is a custom document for that particular invention and covers intellectual property, marketing, and design. After the report is completed, inventors can continue to e-mail questions to him at no charge.

Rather than telling inventors whose inventions he thinks are not marketable to forget their ideas, Lander usually recommends more market research and points out where he anticipates problems will arise.

"I don't want to discourage an inventor," he said, "and I could be wrong." Lander said his process varies based on the stage of development of the client's invention. Some inventors contact him when they already have a patent while others do so at the idea stage. However, Lander encourages inventors to have a marketability or commercial potential assessment done early in the invention process before any money is spent on the invention. Generally, he begins by signing a nondisclosure form and evaluating the invention's marketability.

Lander suggests inventors determine whether trade shows and inventor groups are nonprofit or for-profit and to avoid the for-profit events and groups. He pointed out that the United Inventors' Association website will not accept advertisements from invention assistance firms with bad reputations in the inventor community.

Lander recommended inventors visit industry trade shows whenever possible, walk the floor with their sell sheets, and talk to manufacturers and retailers as a way of researching the industry and making contacts. Often, a visitor can get into a trade show for free with advance registration using nothing more than a business card printed at a copy store. If you receive favorable reactions from tradeshow participants, ask for their cards and call them a few weeks after the show.

"If you go to a trade show for your industry, you will either fall on your face or get somewhere," he said. "It does not leave you wondering."

Lander had a client who invented a product called the BraBall® to protect bras in the washing machine. Before contacting Lander, the client obtained a patent. The inventor was unable to afford the tooling to produce the invention at that time. A competing company saw the patent and designed its own product. The competitor's product was the first one to market.

Lander warns inventors to learn from the BraBall experience. "If you have a niche item the catalogs will not want two of, do not bother with a patent," he said. "Put that money into upgrading the product instead of patenting." *For more information on avoiding patent problems, see Chapter 4.*

To learn more about Lander, read his articles, or contact him, visit his website, **www.inventor-mentor.com**, or e-mail **jack@inventor-mentor. com**.

CHAPTER 2:

Researching Your Idea

"None of my inventions came by accident.
I see a worthwhile need to be met and I
make trial after trial until it comes. What
it boils down to is 1 percent inspiration
and 99 percent perspiration."

— THOMAS EDISON

Whether you have one solid idea or many innovative ideas, you need to do some digging and find out whether your concepts have already hit the market.

Watch for Clues in Everyday Life

Taking note of your personal experiences and watching other people throughout your day will help you identify if there is a need for your product. If you are planning to improve upon a product already on the market, be open-minded when learning about it. It is crucial to figure out a product's advantages and disadvantages first and then try to improve on them. Examine how easy or difficult it is to use the product as it is currently designed. Consider how other people use the product and note whether they have any difficulties. Document each characteristic objectively so you can see what areas need improvement. This information will help build a foundation for you to make the product better or make a new product.

During your research into a product, also take a look at how its manufacturer markets it. Marketing strategy impacts how quickly a product will or will not be successful. *Learn more about marketing in Chapters 12 and 13.*

When you discover details about products you know are successful, you can use similar ideas with your own product design. This includes consumer-friendly ideas, such as using only one or two fonts and color contrasts in order to read the label quickly, and designing the product and packaging to be easy to open and simple to use. Make notes about your observations and use them when it is time to design your own product. *This is discussed further in Chapter 6.*

Despite the millions of handy products already invented, there is still a great need for new inventions to make life more convenient. You surely have come across frustrating problems at home or work, on the road, or anyplace you go as part of your day — even if your only problem is a gadget or a system that has the potential to work better. For example, if you have children, you know when an infant needs to eat, he or she needs to eat immediately. For parents who bottle-feed, bottles are often made up ahead of time out of convenience and stored in the refrigerator. Therefore, a quick bottle-warmer over a microwave might save busy parents some time.

Talk to people

Frustrated consumers can be a great resource — their needs and wants will help lay the groundwork for your creative process.

A good way to start is to make a survey and collect feedback about developing an invention. The type of questions you ask will depend on the stage your idea is in. If you have an idea already and want to get some feedback about it, center your questions on the need your product will fulfill. If you have not decided on an idea, you might be inspired by gathering information about what frustrates people about their daily lives. Carry out your survey with a variety of people from different demographic backgrounds (age, race, education, profession). *See the Appendix for a sample questionnaire.*

Disqualifying Factors

Certain factors will immediately knock your invention right out of consideration, so make sure they will not affect your idea before you start creating. If your idea fits into one of these categories, save yourself time and effort by moving on to another project. Here are some things that automatically will disqualify your invention:

> ➤ It is illegal or violates industry standards or regulations. If this is the case, see whether you can find a way to tweak your product to meet those criteria.

> ➤ It moves an already established company, brand, or product line in a different direction than its current strategy.

> ➤ It requires unproven or expensive equipment or technology. If you can modify your idea to use different equipment or technology that is proven and efficient, you may be able to save your invention.

> ➤ The initial investment outweighs the likelihood of profiting from the invention. To circumvent this, you can try to simplify your invention or use different materials to cut costs.

> ➤ The industry is leapfrogging over your invention's innovation, and it would not increase a company's competitiveness enough to justify taking it to market. For example, creating software that runs on a specific Windows operating system. By the time you have completed research and development, created the software, and met with potential companies, the software may be outdated. If this is the case, try to come up with ways you can make your product more innovative or useful under broader circumstances. Figure out where the industry is moving, and modify your idea to meet those needs. In the example given above, you could adapt your software to run on several operating systems to compensate for the ever-changing digital environment.

Determine the Marketability of Your Idea

Now that you have made sure your idea does not involve any disqualifying factors, you must make sure you have a marketable idea. First, you must determine whether your business or invention is going to make money and whether a market even exists for your product. Then you will have to decide whether you can reach that market.

Not only do you need to have a marketable idea, you also must have a way to market or advertise it. If no one can find you or knows about you or your product, you are not going to sell it. Therefore, make sure you do your research. You do not want spend time and effort on a product that will be impossible for you to market or advertise. A worst-case scenario would be trying to market a product no one is interested in buying. Figuring out marketability now will save you from disaster.

Do a basic Internet search for your product or idea. Although the Internet is not always reliable and you may need to double-check information for accuracy, it is a good place to start. When running your search, you may find other products or ideas similar to yours. They may be offering the same thing you want to provide, even if it is in a different way. If so, you can be fairly certain a market is out there for your idea or product.

To help you in your Internet research, use a meta-search engine. These search tools incorporate more than one search engine for you at once. When you put your query in, you will not be searching only on Google, you also will be searching on Yahoo!, MSN, and other search providers. This is a good timesaver and is effective. The following are some options for meta-search engines:

> Dogpile (**www.dogpile.com**): This site sends a query to a customizable list of search engines.

> Yippy (**http://search.yippy.com**). When you enter a search term, such as "patents," Yippy will return matching responses from the major search engines and also sort the pages into categories.

Checking to see whether any publications, magazines, or newspapers have written about the concept behind your idea or the problem you are trying to solve also will let you know whether a market exists. Finding media coverage is a good sign you are on the right track and have a marketable product or idea. If your product is similar to others, make sure it has a quality that sets it apart.

Determine if Your Idea Is Already Patented

A patent is a property right given to a product's inventor. When you have a patent on a product, the invention is yours, and no one else can make the same product. It also means that if someone holds the patent for the idea you have, your creative process stops.

The United States Patent and Trademark Office (USPTO) issues patents. You do not *have* to do a patent search before applying for a patent, but it is an essential step to ensure you do not waste your time developing an idea that is already patented. Most patented ideas do not become products for sale, so simply conducting an Internet search for your product or going to a store will not paint the full picture. It is far better to find out early in the process whether your product is already patented than to discover this information after you have taken out a loan for manufacturing. You have a few choices when it comes to researching whether your idea or product is already on the market or is in another inventors' development process.

For a patent search, you can: 1) hire a patent attorney; 2) hire a patent searcher; or 3) do it yourself. The first two options require less of your time but cost you more money. This discussion will concentrate on the cost-saving route: the do-it-yourself option. The Internet is a vast arena filled with all the information you will need; you just need to know how to access it. You also can conduct a patent search in person at the USPTO in Arlington, Virginia. If you do not live near Arlington, specialized libraries — referred to as Patent and Trademark Depository Libraries — throughout the United States keep copies of the materials housed in the USPTO. If your idea has not been trademarked or has not had a patent issued for it, you will need to take steps toward making your idea legal and protected. *Chapter 4 will guide you through the process of protecting your intellectual property.*

Search the U.S. Patent and Trademark Office archives

At the beginning of your journey, your head was probably spinning with several ideas. You might have had many different designs or adaptations for the product or idea you want to market. After completing online research, you probably narrowed your ideas down to one or two. Do not get discouraged if your idea is already on the market. If you have a fresh, new take on the idea or product, you still might be able to make those adaptations and find success.

For now, assume your online search did not turn up any registered products similar to your concept. The next step is to check the USPTO's archives. Searching archives is something you can do on your own and with much less expense than hiring someone to search for you. Plus, you can do your research completely online if you do not want to visit Arlington in person. The USPTO offers Web databases you can look through to locate patent information. It also has a search engine you can use. Go to **www.uspto. gov** and search for words related to your idea or product. The USPTO's site provides full-text information about patents dating back to 1976. If you have information about a specific patent, you also might be able to search for older records. Another good site to check is **www.google.com/patents**, which has some patents dating back further than the USPTO.

Patents are broken down into classes and subclasses of inventions. The classification system allows you to investigate patents that fall under the same class as your idea. Start your research in the USPTO's online database by doing keyword searches. Use words and phrases that explain your product or invention and how it works. When you put information into the system, be sure to cover all aspects of the product. Think about your invention or idea for a moment. Consider exactly what it does, what materials it will be made of, and what end result it produces. If you are looking for patents on the BlackBerry®, for example, you might search "smart phone" in addition to "BlackBerry." You also might search "Research in Motion," the developer of the BlackBerry. Or you could search "ARM 7™" or "ARM 9™," the processors used in the BlackBerry.

The online database includes only products patented from 1976 onward unless you know the exact number of the patent, the date it was issued, or the current U.S. classification. If you have that information, you can search back to 1790. If you do not have specific information but think your idea or invention could have been patented before 1976, you will need to visit a Patent and Trademark Depository Library. There are 80 of these depositories throughout the United States, and they will have detailed information concerning patents filed before 1976.

After you have done your keyword search, your results — the patent numbers and titles of all works matching the keywords you used — will appear. Click on the resulting titles to go to the complete information page about the patent. This information will give you a clear understanding about the inventions or ideas you found with your keyword search. When you open the individual results, you will see a description of the patented item; information about prior art, drawings/figures of the patented product; the names of the investors, patent examiners and attorney/agent/firm; the claims made in the patent; and the class of the patent, among other things.

You also might need to research trademarks when going through the USPTO archives. A trademark is a word, symbol, or name used to label or set apart a manufacturer or seller's idea or goods from those manufactured or sold by others. If you want to call your idea or invention by a specific title or name, you will need to file a trademark application. First, make sure the trademark is not currently in use. The steps in searching for a registered trademark are the same as searching for an existing patent. Trademarks are registered in the same office as patents, and you can search for them using the online databases from the USPTO.

At this point, you may find that your idea has already been produced. This happens frequently. More than 350,000 patent applications are filed with the USPTO every year. Those numbers break down into many inventions and ideas. Some of them are duplicates. This is why it is important to start the creative process by researching your idea before you get too far along with development and to document the process of your invention. If one inventor can prove he or she came up with the idea first, that inventor will have preference over the other.

Conduct a Preliminary Market Analysis and Invention Assessment

What you need to obtain next are a market analysis and an invention assessment. These tools will let you know how profitable your product or idea has the potential to be. Some companies will sell you only a market analysis (without the invention assessment) because it usually will show better statistics. A market analysis does give you some good insight about the market for your product, but it does not tell you anything about whether your invention is potentially *marketable* in that market. You can, of course, research and calculate your own market analysis, but there are a few reasons why this is not advisable. For one, you, as the inventor, will be biased toward your invention. Also, you may not have the business and marketing background these companies specialize in. You could ask friends to try conducting a market analysis, but if you want the most realistic possible assessment, a specialist is your best bet.

Market analysis

A **market analysis** is an examination of the market for your product. It offers an overview of the market that includes products similar to yours. The information you want to see in a market analysis includes a breakdown of competitors, sales statistics for similar products, use of similar products, sales expectations, market size, market growth rate, market profitability, target customers, manufacturing costs, key success factors, and industry trends. The market analysis will give you a picture of the commercial environment your product will enter. Although this analysis is important, it is only part of the whole picture. You also must find out whether there is a need for your product or idea, or you will find yourself at a loss.

Invention assessment

An **invention assessment**, also known as an invention evaluation or product evaluation, assesses your product or idea to determine its worthiness in the market. This step helps you figure out whether your product will be well received by the public. An invention assessment has two main purposes: to find out whether it is worthwhile to invest more money developing a specific idea and to provide facts you can use to impress a potential investor or buyer when you try to raise money, sell your product, or license your idea. Keep in mind that only a small percentage of inventions make a profit.

Many invention promotion firms are ready to help you with these assessments. Be sure you are choosing a reliable firm to conduct your invention assessment. Some disreputable promoters prey on novice inventors. One red flag is when firms ask for fees upfront. These companies will tell you your idea is a winner, charge you heavily for their research and marketing, and offer you additional services — for additional fees.

If you are interested in working with an invention promotion firm, take some precautions before signing an agreement and paying the promoter any amount of money. In the beginning of your discussions with company representatives, ask for the details on the total cost of their services. If you sense any hesitation from them, take it as a warning sign. Dishonest promoters take advantage of your interest in your invention. They may even urge you to patent your invention before it is ready and might give you false hope about your product's market potential.

Sample market analysis and invention assessment

To better understand the difference between a market analysis and invention assessment, review the reports below. This is an analysis of a fictional product called the Burpee Baby Bottle, a baby bottle that eliminates gas passed on to the baby drinking from it through the bottle's air-releasing mechanism.

Market Analysis

➤ 1 million baby bottles were sold in 2009.

➤ Baby bottles are expected to top $17.5 million in 2011.

➤ The average price for a baby bottle set in 2009 was $12.

➤ The average cost to manufacture a baby bottle was $1.

Invention Assessment

➤ Most consumers want their baby bottle to eliminate gas.

➤ More than 360 different competitive products are in the baby bottle industry.

➢ The Burpee Baby Bottle is heavier than and more expensive than most others, so it is less desirable for consumers.

➢ The Burpee Baby Bottle is more complex to use than other baby bottles.

➢ Consumers of baby bottles do not change types of bottles easily.

If you look only at the market analysis, it seems the Burpee Baby Bottle would be a good invention to produce and market. Once you consider the invention assessment, you can ascertain many additional points that will be essential to your decision on whether to pursue this idea. In this example, it is clear that the Burpee Baby Bottle would not be a good invention to invest in because it does not offer an improved product consumers would pay to have. For this idea to be successful, you would need to make some modifications.

Invention Evaluation Organizations

Another way to get an unbiased opinion about your product's commercialization potential is to ask a legitimate invention evaluation organization. Invention marketing scams abound, but good guys are out there; you just have to look for them. Your best bet is to use a nonprofit group, government agency, or university service that charges on a fee-for-service basis and has no vested interest in your success. Examples of these organizations include:

➢ Washington State University Innovation Assessment Center: Invention evaluation and, for selected inventions, design and marketing assistance. (**www.business.wsu.edu/organizations/iac/ Pages/inventor.aspx**)

➤ Wisconsin Innovation Center at the University of Wisconsin at Whitewater: Invention evaluation and marketing expansion opportunities for innovative manufacturers, technology businesses, and independent inventors. (**http://wisc.uww.edu**)

➤ WIN Innovation Center at Southwest Missouri State University in Springfield's Center for Business and Economic Development: A variety of inventor services including invention evaluation. (**www.wini2.com**)

➤ United Inventors Association Innovation Assessment Program: Invention evaluation using a structured evaluation method for $300. (**www.uiausa.com**)

➤ Baugh Center for Entrepreneurship at Baylor University: Invention evaluation service provided at a fee that covers expenses. It established the first nongovernment-funded innovation evaluation program in 1981. (**www.baylor.edu/business/entrepreneur**)

➤ Buchnell University's Small Business Development Center, housed in the university's engineering school: Assists Pennsylvania-based inventors in creating new products and exporting products, provides patent assistance, and helps inventors find markets for their products. (**www.bucknell.edu/x8122.xml**)

➤ Maine Patent Program at the University of Maine School of Law: Invention evaluation and assistance for Maine residents only. (**www.tlc.usm.maine.edu**)

➤ Public Interest Intellectual Property Advisors: Advice for inventors seeking to promote projects in the developing world. (**www.piipa.org**)

➤ National Institute of Justice's Office of Law Enforcement Technology Commercialization: Assistance for inventors of technology with law enforcement or corrections applications. (**http://mockprisonriot. org/mpr/index.aspx**)

➢ Canadian Innovation Centre: Assistance with Canadian patents; also guides inventors on getting their products on the market. (**www.innovationcentre.ca**)

Beware of scams

The organizations listed above are all universities, government agencies, or nonprofit groups you can trust when looking for an invention evaluation. Some of these organizations will evaluate your invention idea for free, while others may charge a minimal fee. For-profit organizations offering to evaluate your invention could be scams. *For more about this topic, see Chapter 14.*

When it is time for you to determine your product's market potential, be cautious because invention promoters might misguide you. These promoters use sales tactics; if you respond to their advertisement, they will try to get details about you and your invention so they can work the information to their advantage. Some firms may even offer you a free preliminary market review. Then they might tell you a market evaluation is necessary to assess your idea — for a fee. They may not perform a genuine market evaluation. Firms only after your money will not give you an honest assessment of your product, its technical feasibility, or market potential. They may tell you they have relationships with manufacturers that might have interest in licensing your invention. According to the Federal Trade Commission, many of these "unscrupulous" firms advertise on television, radio, the Internet, and in print publications, and they will provide a toll-free number for you to call.

Is Your Product or Idea Truly in Demand?

It is important to understand what "in demand" really means in the marketplace. Demand is the desire of purchasers, consumers, clients, or employers for a particular commodity, service, or other item. It is dependent upon consumers and the purchases they are willing to make. The more you learn about what consumers do and do not demand, the easier it will be for you to create something they want. Making an in-demand product is more about a concept than the product itself. Ask yourself what consumers want and why. To continue with the example of the Burpee Baby Bottle, do consumers want an innovation in baby bottles? You may think it is a good idea, but do people need a baby bottle with a mechanism for eliminating gas? Would they be willing to pay their hard-earned money for your high-end baby bottle that could cost more than a traditional baby bottle?

Once you think you are on the right path to creating a marketable product, focus on how quickly and efficiently you can transfer your idea from your head to consumers' hands. Say you have decided the Burpee Baby Bottle would be received well by consumers. Now, how quickly can you transform your idea into a product? Consumers' desires change frequently, so you have to create a well-organized plan, no matter what the product is. Will your product be outdated by the time it hits store shelves? This is an especially important question when dealing with electronics and technology. If your idea falls into those categories, here are some tips:

> ➢ The product will probably be expensive to produce, so be thorough in your market and invention analysis. If it seems like a risk, assess the product carefully to make sure you are ready to put forth the time, effort, and money to bring it to fruition.

➤ Be sure there is no similar idea out there, or, if there is, be sure your product truly is superior in an aspect such as design, affordability, or performance.

➤ Do everything in your power to make sure manufacturers produce your product as soon as possible because technology changes quickly.

There is no set age group that most often uses in-demand or hip new products. Customers span from teenagers to people in their mid-40s to the more senior population or younger children, so be open-minded as you analyze opinions from people who fit these demographics. As you read responses to your market-survey questions, stay focused on the information as it pertains to inventing or helping improve a product. Do not criticize or pass judgment; just objectively document relevant information from the responses you receive. This step will take considerable time, but these surveys will help you discover and target the people who will buy your in-demand products. They are the ones you need to listen to. Again, when seeking consumer opinions, be careful not to give away too much information about your invention lest someone steal your idea before you have a chance to protect it.

Creative, researched ideas are the most important part of being successful in the marketplace when it comes to in-demand products. Ensure that your research covers the conceptual and the marketing components of your project.

Tips: Research is the Key

Study other people's successful marketing techniques so you can succeed quickly as well.

➤ Learn how other in-demand products are successful.

> Reproduce these products' successes in terms of when to advertise to potential consumers, what language is best, and what is and is not included in your marketing and labeling.

> Study the most successful layout designs — online and in print — and other marketing platforms that get messages about products out to the consumer faster.

Whether your invention will be a success really depends on how practical it is. Ask yourself these questions:

> How much will people use this invention?

> How easy is it going to be to understand?

> Will people relate to the product and see a purpose for it?

You can invent everything from workout equipment and hair accessories to bathroom gadgets and kitchen appliances, but in the end, your product or service must fill a need. The more practical the invention is, the simpler it might make a person's everyday life. The only way you will make money from your invention is if there is a need for it among consumers. In order to ensure your invention's success, you must do some basic research at the start of the process, and you cannot be afraid to try. If your product or idea seems like a practical solution to you, you can bet it will benefit someone else's life, too. The key is research.

Action Steps

Research products in the industry that are similar to your idea — these will be your competition in the market. You can create an Excel spreadsheet or a table in Word and keep track of information about those related products. For each similar product answer the following questions:

> How is the product similar to your idea? For example, does it fulfill the same need as your invention?

> How is the product different from your idea? For example, is it more complex than your idea?

> What types of materials are used on the product?

> How is the product manufactured? Who manufactures it?

> How is the product distributed? Is it sold online only? In specialty stores? In big box stores?

> Are there any common customer complaints about the product?

> What is the pricing for the product? This will be useful later in the process of creating your invention.

> How are the sales of the product? Is it a major player in the industry?

> Does the product have any intellectual property protections, such as trademarks or patents?

There may be other things to note that relate specifically to your product, such as features. Be sure to write those things down as well. You can also update this as you go.

CASE STUDY: KNIFE AND FORK LIFT™

Thomas Madden
www.knifeandforklift.com

Thomas Madden was eating too much. Like many people, he was eating too fast and not giving his brain enough time to let him know he was full. His invention, the Knife and Fork Lift, is what he describes as "a combination of dumbbells and utensils. From each of two stainless steel dumbbells, a knife and a fork extend from the ends, so when lifting food from your plate, you are actually doing curls with these 1.5 lb forks and knives. You are, in effect, exercising while eating."

STEPS IN THE PROCESS

Madden first designed a prototype of the utensils based on the image he had in his head. Once he was satisfied with his prototype, he sent it to Chinese manufacturers to get quotes on costs of manufacturing. The process of finalizing the design was lengthy. The manufacturer designed and sent a sample, and Madden would examine and make changes. Eventually, Madden approved the design and the Knife and Fork Lift began to be manufactured. Six weeks after approving the final design, he received his first shipment by air, and a larger shipment by sea later. Altogether, the process took about six months and cost $20,000.

Madden believed being the first to market was more important than obtaining a patent. He also believed his name for the product would set him above any competitors that might enter the market.

MARKETING AND PUBLICITY

Madden created a website called **www.knifeandforklift.com**. In addition, he hired a public relations firm to generate publicity. In November 2009, the Knife and Fork Lift was featured on the *Today Show* on NBC and in an article in the *Los Angeles Times*. After that, Madden and his Knife and Fork Lift were featured on numerous shows. This is one example of how a new and original idea can be turned into a successful business endeavor through the proper manufacturing process. But it also shows how much publicity goes into one little 1.5-pound product.

Chapter 3:
Protecting
Your Idea

"I believe in human dignity as the source of national purpose, human liberty as the source of national action, the human heart as the source of national compassion, and in the human mind as the source of our invention and our ideas."

— JOHN F. KENNEDY

Intellectual property is an idea, invention, method, formula, procedure, or process that has fiscal value. Because of the potential value of your intellectual property — the idea for your invention — it is essential that you protect it. These types of protections are methods for proving or legally confirming ownership of the ideas, words, and concepts that make up your invention.

What Intellectual Property Protection Can and Cannot Do

Your idea for an invention, say, the Burpee Baby Bottle, is your intellectual property. Protecting intellectual property involves a variety of procedures for making inventions, ideas, words, and concepts proprietary. **Proprietary concepts** include patents, trademarks, copyrights, trade secrets, and secrecy. It gives you the right to use your invention without compensating others and allows you to prevent others from using it without compensating you; that is all it does. It will not make your invention profitable, though lack of it may — or may not — prevent you from profiting from your invention.

Intellectual property protection is a legal tool, not magic fairy dust. The more you know about it, the less mystical it will seem and the better you will be at devising a strategy that combines commercialization and intellectual property protection. When your invention is proprietary, it is your property, owned and controlled by you.

Naive idealists that we are, inventors tend to feel that obtaining an intellectual property (IP) protection such as a patent confers a status of "real" inventor on us. This is not only a mistaken idea, but also an expensive one. Obtaining a patent before developing a commercialization strategy can endanger the profits you seek to earn from your invention by providing others who are quicker to commercialize your idea public notice of your invention. Obtaining a patent outside of a fully developed commercialization strategy is just as foolhardy as telling everyone you meet about your invention idea.

To benefit from IP protections, you must develop a strategy that combines such protections with commercialization so you, the inventor, have a legal monopoly on something unique and desirable. To position yourself in that way, first examine and package your intellectual property assets by asking the following questions:

> What are the unique things about your invention? These could become the basis for utility patent claims, trade secrets, or marketable know-how. For instance, how does the Burpee Baby Bottle differ from other bottles on the market?

> What design features set your invention apart from the competition? Does it have a certain heft and shape to a handle or pedal, a contemporary look to a knob or casing, or a certain style that, while nonfunctional, creates affection for your product? These aesthetic features can be the basis for design patents.

> What logos, trade names, graphics, or brand identifiers have you developed to build a brand association in consumers' minds? These materials may be eligible for trademark protection.

> What written materials, be they handbooks, manuals, marketing materials, or articles about your ideas, have you written? These materials can, and should, be copyrighted.

> What specialized knowledge do you have that can make manufacturing, distributing, or marketing your invention more successful? This is the basis for marketable know-how — consulting time for which you can charge a prospective licensee.

Keep Your Idea Confidential

One of the most difficult parts of the inventing process is keeping your idea under wraps. You are undoubtedly excited about your idea's potential. You may want to share it with anyone who will listen because you hope to make people as excited as you are. You also might want to get feedback from friends, coworkers, or family members. At this point, try to keep your idea to yourself. If you decide to discuss your idea with anyone, have that person sign a confidentiality or nondisclosure agreement. *See an example in the Appendix.*

The confidentiality agreement should include all the information about the idea for your invention. You want the document to be comprehensive and detailed. If you discuss your idea without a confidentiality agreement, it is considered public disclosure under patent law. Under such law, you have one year from public disclosure to apply for a patent. *This is further discussed in Chapter 4.*

You might feel uncomfortable asking people to sign the agreement, especially if you are working with a friend or family member. You must protect your idea, however, so have even your spouse, significant other, or children sign one. If you are enlisting anyone's help with brainstorming, research, design, or any other aspect of the invention before you file a patent application, have that person sign a confidentiality agreement. Once you file for a patent, the confidentiality agreement is no longer necessary. Your patent application protects you from disclosure. If you want further protection, however, you can still have people sign a confidentiality agreement.

The inventor's notebook

One way to protect your idea is to keep good records of your entire thought process. By keeping a signed and dated documentation of each step, you afford yourself security. This is not a form of patent protection itself, but it will help if another inventor formulates the same invention or tries to steal your idea. The USPTO will compare your records with the other inventor's records to determine who had the idea first.

Begin your inventor's log with a date and description of your idea and how you came up with it. Sign and date each page and each separate entry in the log. A bound notebook enables you to document a chain of events and ideas that occurred in a plausible, chronological sequence. Loose-leaf material does not permit building the same sort of case — nor can you organize it easily. Your notebook should contain descriptive narrative, drawings, calculations, equations, formulas, and any other materials that constitute your invention or a description of your invention. Each time you improve on the idea, document that event and how you developed it, along with your signature and date. For example, with the Burpee Baby Bottle, you may have numerous sketches and designs after realizing the previous design is not functional or would cost too much to manufacture. In your notebook, keep detailed notes about the process by which you get to your final product.

In addition to your detailed records, it is also beneficial to have two or three witnesses document their observations of your invention process. Once the idea is fairly developed, have the witness sign a nondisclosure agreement and witness statement that describes the invention and its uses. The witness statement can include a drawing or sketch. It also should include language attesting that the witness has read the description and understands the invention's purpose and workings. The witness should sign the confidentiality or nondisclosure agreement before you show him or her the invention, and then he or she should read, sign, and date the witness statement. The witnesses you choose should not be related to you or have had any part in developing the invention. Choose witnesses with knowledge or expertise in the realm of your invention. If that is not an option, use someone who is not a relative or a co-inventor — just be sure the person understands the invention. You also want these witnesses to be credible in the event you have to go to court over your product.

You have now established what is known as **priority**, meaning you can prove the date on which you had the idea for your invention. If others claim they came up with it first, you have materials that back up and verify your claim to the invention. After refining and researching your invention, you want to be sure it remains yours. Your vision for the invention is valuable, and others might try to copy it.

For an inventor who has priority, intellectual property protection offers the right to profit from the invention in commerce; this right is enforceable in civil court. This means that to stop others from infringing on your rights and profiting from your invention without your permission, you have to take legal action if a problem arises. The burden is on you to go after anyone who infringes on your intellectual property.

There are several types of formal intellectual property protections, each of which has different features, including rights conferred, aspects of the invention that are protected, requirements for protection, and length of protection. Normally, inventions will be eligible for more than one type of protection. *See Chapter 4 to learn more about formal protection opportunities.*

It is important to take steps right at the start of the process to ensure your idea stays yours. Your idea is your property, and the following section will explain the steps you should take to protect it.

CASE STUDY: SUPER SQUARES FOOTBALL GAME

Ryan Weber
www.biggamesportscards.com

Ryan Weber always loved putting together football square pools for big games, such as the Super Bowl. A football square pool lays out 100 squares in chart form (ten vertical and ten horizontal) that coordinate with the two teams playing. Betters buy a square based on the last number of each team's score (with choices from zero to nine) and place their initials in it, so it is easy for anyone to play and win even if they do not understand the game. Weber wanted a way to do football pools for the regular games as well — and with a lot fewer people. In a few months, Weber created the Super Squares Football Game, a pre-printed football pool. It was cheap to produce, and he felt there was at least a demand that would meet his costs, so he knew it was a viable idea to patent.

Weber said with the new layout, he could play the game anywhere and with anyone, including a group of about five to 20 friends, family members, co-workers, or even strangers he met at sporting establishments.

THE FIRST STEPS

Weber's first step in creating his invention was to contact a local patent attorney who conducted a product and patent search. After the search, they then filed a provisional patent application and filed a utility (non-provisional) patent application. A provisional patent is less expensive and less complicated than a utility patent, but the utility patent offers more protection. "We felt that our product is unique yet can be challenged," Weber said. "We want the protection so we can really see the entire lifespan of it and don't want to see other 'knockoffs' on the market."

MANUFACTURING

Weber partnered with a manufacturer in the United States to directly oversee production and make changes and corrections when necessary. "These are all important to maintain the integrity of the idea," he said. "Once you allow this step to be taken over by others, the idea may be at risk, as only the creator knows how the product needs to be presented. I believe we made the right decision because of the success we've had so far. We are a young company and have already sold products all over the country."

To get the Super Squares Football Game to market, Ryan estimated that his out-of-pockets expenses were about $3,000 — including production costs, marketing (including promos and giveaways), and mailings.

THE EVOLUTION

Weber recently launched Big Game Sports Cards, Inc., which sells game squares for different sporting events. The products are sold through the company's website (**www.biggamesportscards.com**). Weber saw a need for something simple to create, and he met it. This is how many great inventions are created: through the perseverance of a viable idea.

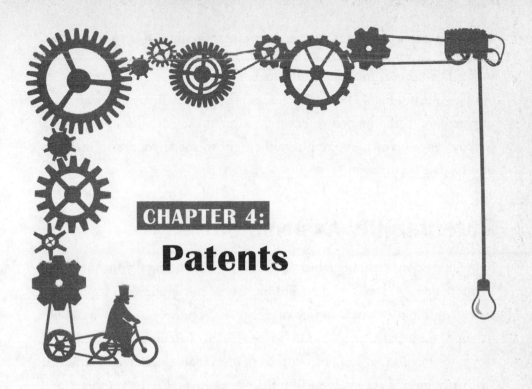

CHAPTER 4:

Patents

"I do not think there is any thrill that can go through the human heart like that felt by the inventor as he sees some creation of the brain unfolding to success.... Such emotions make a man forget food, sleep, friends, love, everything."

— NIKOLA TESLA, SERBIAN INVENTOR

A **patent** is a property right given to the inventor of a product. The U.S. Patent and Trademark Office (USPTO) grants patents in the United States. Owning the patent for a product means you own the rights to the product, and no one else can make or use it during the time period in which the patent is valid. Patents provide protection within the country it is issued. In the United States, this protection lasts for 14 years, depending on when the patent application was filed and the priority of the claim, and the patent cannot be renewed once it has expired. Patents are personal property you can sell or license. Alone, patents do not prevent others from making or selling your product. The USPTO does not enforce the patent; you must be attentive to the market to ensure no one makes or sells your product without your permission. You have the right to sue anyone who infringes upon a patent you own.

Patentability Assessment

Some inventions are patentable; others are not. Deciding if your invention is patentable will save you time and money — the application fee and the cost of hiring a patent attorney or agent — because you will know not to apply for a patent that is sure to be denied. Patents are the strongest form of intellectual property protection available. Knowing whether your invention is patentable will influence your intellectual property and commercialization strategies. Remember, a patent is not a requirement for commercializing a product. Even though you might not be able to get a patent, it does not mean you cannot still design, make, market, sell, or license your product. Although a professional patentability assessment is wise before you spend the time and money, smart inventors complete their own informal assessment first.

Informal patentability assessment

Model your informal assessment after the method patent examiners follow. Patent examiners look at several factors when deciding whether to issue a patent. This discussion will begin with the lowest hurdle and move to the highest.

USEFULNESS

As the name implies, utility patents must first be useful. Design patents, on the other hand, do not necessarily have to be more useful, just new and aesthetically pleasing. If the invention has no real-world application — perhaps it is the physical embodiment of a fancy idea that looks nice but does nothing — it does not qualify for a utility patent, but it may qualify for a design patent. *Look back at your assessment from Chapter 2 to determine the purpose of your invention.* If an invention does not work or does not serve its intended purpose — no matter how good the idea is and how nice the product looks — a patent examiner would deem it not useful. Also, the use described in the patent application must be legal and not primarily intended for fraudulent or deceptive purposes.

NOVELTY

The next hurdle a patent examiner will look for is novelty. To be novel, all the components of your invention together must not have been described anywhere before. The Burpee Baby Bottle would be a novel idea unless there is another bottle with the same purpose and the same design. Patent examiners, patent attorneys, and other patent professionals use the term **prior art** to refer to any existing information an examiner may use to judge the novelty of your invention.

Prior art includes:

> ➢ All previous patents
> ➢ Any publicly known, used, or disclosed information in the United States that precedes the inventor's documented date of coming up with the idea for the invention
> ➢ An earlier invention by someone else
> ➢ Your invention itself, if it was publicly disclosed more than 12 months prior to the patent application

➤ Any literature or publication relating to your invention in any language made public before your date of invention or more than 12 months prior to the patent application, including: corporate brochures, trade journals, magazines, academic publications, and any document available in any library anywhere in the world

Based on this list, the novelty hurdle may seem insurmountable. Remember: The prior art of your invention would include all the claims you will make regarding your invention. Claims establish the unique features of the invention. Novelty does not have to be substantial to qualify. A minor variation on prior art is sufficient to pass a patent examination. Physical differences, new combinations of old materials or components, or new uses for existing items all meet the novelty standard.

OBVIOUSNESS

The biggest hurdle an inventor must pass to be granted a utility patent is the requirement that your invention is not obvious to someone in the pertinent field. This requirement involves a thorough experiment on the part of the patent examiner, who must determine what field your invention falls into and whether your invention would be obvious to a theoretical person who has an average amount of knowledge and skill in that field and is aware of all prior art in the field.

Courts have established a body of patent law that provides guidance on obviousness. This standard will be met if your invention meets one of these two primary criteria: 1) It involves an original insight, or 2) it produces unexpected results. If neither of these is the case, do not despair; you can combine secondary criteria to make your invention unobvious. They are not secondary in importance, only secondary after the first two have not been met. These secondary factors include:

➤ Resolving a long-standing problem in the field

- Making an invention work that others have failed to make work
- Modifying an existing invention by omitting one of its primary elements and retaining its effectiveness
- Creating a new feature that enhances the invention's utility
- Accomplishing what had been thought impossible
- Constituting a commercial success while not violating the 12-month rule

STRENGTH OF CLAIM

In addition to meeting the utility, novelty, and obviousness tests, also assess whether you can make your invention's patent claims strong enough to withstand competitors' efforts to engineer around the patent. There is no point in investing in a patent that will not be approved or one so generic that it would not offer much protection, even if approved. Additionally, you must continually amend patents to reflect innovations and developments that improve your invention. If your intellectual property rights are limited to the point where they do not offer real protection from competition, your ability to license or sell your invention or attract investors will be harmed.

To qualify for a patent, your invention must be unique. Patent examiners, government employees of the USPTO, will search prior art to ensure nothing like your claims has been made public before. The patent examiner is the third step of the patent search. Before your application reaches the examiner, make sure you have conducted two prior art searches of your own: a preliminary search on your own and a professional search by either a patent attorney or patent agent.

You are not required to conduct a patent search before filing an application, but it makes a lot of sense. Patent applications are difficult, time-consuming, and often costly. If any prior art exists on your invention, the examiner will reject your application. Find out whether there is bad news out there before you go to the trouble of applying.

Anyone can conduct a search of prior art, but not everyone can do it well. Such searches are subjective by their nature. No two examiners will come up with the same results. That said, most capable examiners will come up with similar results. By conducting your own search, you can save yourself money and learn about your market, the competition, and the likelihood of your invention being patentable.

Types of Patents

The three types of patents in the United States are utility patents, design patents, and plant patents. *See the Appendix for a detailed chart comparing these types.* Utility patents are the most common and protect an invention's unique functional elements. New machines or improvements on existing products fall under utility patents. These patents are issued for 20 years, beginning with the application filing date. The inventor also must pay periodic maintenance fees at 3.5 years, 7.5 years, and 11.5 years. For small entities, such as independent inventors or small businesses, the fees will be smaller than for larger companies. Here is a breakdown of the 2009 fees:

> **3.5 years:** $490 for small entities and $980 for others
>
> **7.5 years:** $1,240 for small entities and $2,480 for others
>
> **11.5 years:** $2,055 for small entities and $4,110 for others

The current fees can be found at the USPTO website (**www.uspto.gov/main/howtofees.htm**), as they are subject to change.

Utility patents protect inventions of the following:

> **New processes:** A new way to do something

- ➢ **New machines**: A new product that does something
- ➢ **New manufactured articles:** Taking raw materials to compose a new product; for example, a chair made of wood shaped to form something new
- ➢ **A new combination of materials or chemicals:** Mixing two or more materials or chemicals to form something new
- ➢ **Improvements:** Making an existing (patented or unpatented) invention better
- ➢ **Combination:** Any two or more of the above five categories

When you apply for a utility patent, you must submit your invention in one of the first five categories listed above. The Burpee Baby Bottle could fall under the utility patent as a new machine. However, depending on the invention, you may want to apply for multiple types of patents, such as a utility patent and a design patent. This will depend on your particular idea.

Design patents protect the invention's unique aesthetic or design elements as well as the appearance of a product. Examples of objects protected by design patents are baby bottles, handbags, and computer icons. If the Burpee Baby Bottle has a unique design, such as an hourglass shape or triangular shape, you could apply for a design patent to protect its appearance. Some objects covered by design patents are also covered by copyrights, for example, the way words and shapes are arranged on paper. If your invention has a unique design but also serves a function, apply for a utility patent instead of a design patent. The Burpee Baby Bottle is a uniquely shaped baby bottle that prevents gas in babies. Even though the design of the Burpee Baby Bottle is unique, it also has a unique function, so you should apply for a utility patent for this invention.

Plant patents protect new varieties of plants. According to the USPTO, a plant patent is granted to an inventor who has "invented or discovered and asexually reproduced a distinct and new variety of plant."

Each of these patents requires proof that the invention is useful, novel, and based on specific, descriptive claims you submit in the application. The following websites can help you decide which patent type to apply for:

> About.com: **http://inventors.about.com/od/provisionalpatent/a/ Provisional_Pat.htm**

> Intellectual Property Law Firms: **www.intellectualpropertylawfirms. com/resources/intellectual-property/patents/patent-types.htm**

> ExpertLaw®: **www.expertlaw.com/library/intellectual_property/ patent_law.html#3**

The one-year rule

Inventors have one year to patent an invention after it is publicly disclosed. If other intellectual property protections are not in place, anyone — not just the inventor — can patent the invention within 12 months of it becoming public. This is not to recommend that you try patenting others' ideas. Instead, be cautious whom you tell about your invention and under what circumstances. There is always the chance someone could patent it before you. Although you have a confidentiality or nondisclosure to protect your idea, individuals you discuss your idea with should be few in number. Beyond witnesses, the prototype designer, the firm you hire to do your invention assessment (if any), one or two experts in the field, and perhaps a patent agent or attorney, no one else needs to know until you have a licensee ready to hear your pitch.

You may inadvertently start the clock ticking on the one-year rule if you discuss your invention with someone who might be in a position to buy it, and you do not have that person sign a confidentiality agreement and a statement saying he or she understands your discussion is not an offer for sale. You want to pursue patenting only as part of a combined commercialization and intellectual property strategy. If you unintentionally start the clock because of public disclosure, it could force you to apply for a patent before you are ready. Filing for a patent is a complex process, and doing it too early could result in your application being denied.

When Is It Worth Pursuing a Patent?

Patent applications are expensive, complicated, and uncertain. How do inventors know when it is worth pursuing a patent? This depends on the intersection of two factors: the patent's profit-enhancing capability and the invention's life cycle. The main question is whether the patent adds to the owner or licensee's profits. A patent can lead to higher profits by maintaining a monopoly on some factor of an invention that increases profitability. Profitability rises by either adding features and benefits, or by decreasing the cost of production or liability. The patent can protect this monopoly unless another inventor engineers around it. It is possible for a competitor to make a product similar enough for customers to relate to yours but different enough that it does not infringe upon your patent. So, even when a patent can boost profits, the real question is this: Will it increase profits enough to exceed the cost of obtaining and maintaining the patent?

Before you can profit from an invention, you must calculate all the costs involved in bringing it to market. How long will it take without a patent for you to make back your investment? Consider the cost of a patent. For a do-it-yourself utility patent, the fees paid to the USPTO for the application, research, examination, and issuance are $1,300 for a small entity, plus $3,785 for maintenance fees throughout the life of the patent, for a total of $5,085. (For other entities, the fees are $2,600 for the application, research, examination, and issuance, and $7,570 for maintenance fees, for a grand total of $10,170.) How long will it take to make back the money? If that time is longer than the product's life cycle, a patent is not worth the investment.

An invention's life cycle is determined by how long it can retain market share in the face of competitor reactions and the entry of new products or technologies into the market. Market share is the percent of a market held by a company. For example, hypothetically, Pepsi™ and Coca-Cola® each retain about 50 percent of the dark soda market. They compete to gain the majority of the market. Or, sticking with the example of the Burpee Baby Bottle, it is not unique in the market — other bottles are available to consumers — but this one is better because of its ability to eliminate gas through its air-releasing mechanism.

Consider the competition when deciding to pursue a patent. To continue with the example, once Burpee Baby Bottle hits store shelves, competitors will determine the success of the product. If it captures a significant market share, competitors will make a similar product. Will the Burpee Baby Bottle have captured enough of the market to hold on to its niche when the competition hits? What will happen when someone introduces a new bottle that outperforms the Burpee Baby Bottle? These are the factors that impact product life cycle, or how long your product is profitable and viable.

A patent on any invention is worthwhile to the extent that its ability to increase profits exceeds its cost during its life cycle. In addition to these considerations, think long and hard about whether your invention design is finalized. A patent on an interim design is unlikely to offer protection if you alter the design. Such a patent does not have much value to a licensee. Finalize your patent claims only when you are certain you have finalized your invention design.

Types of Patent Applications

Although you can apply for a patent without a lawyer, it is highly advisable that you get some legal backup. A lawyer specializing in patents will know the ins and outs of the process and help you speed it along successfully.

Provisional applications

You can submit a provisional patent application to the USPTO before officially applying. For a fee of $110 for small entities ($220 for all others), you can establish your priority date for less money and with less paperwork than a regular patent application. No patent is issued with a provisional application; instead, it protects your rights to the invention in the event someone else submits an application for the same invention. The **provisional patent application** contains a description of the invention but does not include the legal claims required for a regular patent application. Submitting a provisional application permits you to claim patent pending for your invention, even if you have no plans to pursue a patent.

You can turn the provisional application into a regular patent application within one year of the original application date. During this one-year period, you can continue to research your product and its potential for success, but with added protection for a small fee. The provisional application is a great option for inventions that are not completely developed. You will have priority rights for the invention and will have the option to make changes or improvements before officially applying for a patent. If two or more inventors try to patent the same invention, the USPTO will consider the application of the inventor with the earliest date of conception. Make sure to consult a patent lawyer or another expert on the wording of your invention and submit a provisional patent sooner rather than later to prevent this from happening.

To help you decide on the matter, here are some pros and cons to a provisional application.

Pros:

> ➤ Claim of "patent pending" makes it more difficult for others to claim your idea
> ➤ Gives you a year to improve upon and make changes to your invention
> ➤ Only a small fee for more intellectual property protection

Cons:

> ➤ Starts the one-year clock to file for a regular patent, if you plan on it
> ➤ Discloses information about your idea

A provisional application should include the USPTO's form and fee and should have a thorough description of the invention, including an explanation of the components, how to make it, and its function. Drawings or sketches might illustrate how it is made or used. Your description must meet two criteria:

> ➤ It must provide sufficient information to instruct the average person experienced in the field on how to make and use the product.
> ➤ It must describe what you see as your ideal or preferred mode for creating and using the product.

Without meeting these two tests, your provisional application does not protect you. Providing accurate and adequate details in the provisional application also gives you further protection should another inventor apply for a patent for the same invention. If your description is insufficient, you will not be able to use the filing date to prove your priority in the event someone else submits an application for the same invention. In addition, a good description will make the transition to an official patent application much easier.

The provisional patent is simple to obtain because it is not examined for merit; the application remains on file and allows the owner to use "Patent Pending" on his or her product. Applying for a provisional utility patent establishes your priority in case someone else submits a later application for the same invention. It also establishes a date by which prior art will be judged. For instance, if someone discusses such an invention in public — even without filing a patent application — your idea would not be patentable unless you can prove you thought of it before this prior art. If you do not adequately describe how to make and use your invention, it may not be sufficient to establish priority or predate prior art. You may want to use an attorney to review or draft this description, but this would lessen the cost benefits of the provisional application.

To receive a regular patent, you must have reduced your invention to practice. Practice is a technical term meaning you must prove it works by making your invention. A provisional application is considered a placeholder if you are unable to reduce your invention to practice by creating a model or prototype. There are some caveats to the provisional patent application, and this is one of them.

Remember: After you start that 12-month clock, if you fail to submit a regular patent application by the end of that period, you have disqualified your invention for patenting. You also could disqualify it for foreign patenting after 12 months, which will be discussed later in this chapter.

Filing a provisional application starts the clock ticking on the USPTO's 18-months between application and disclosure. If you use the provisional application process and then file a regular application in 12 months, you have six months before your invention's description is made public. If you file only a regular application, you have a total of 18 months before the competition can learn your invention's particulars.

If you significantly improve, change, or redesign your invention in the time between the provisional and regular application, your provisional application may not qualify as having adequately disclosed the invention you are claiming in your regular application. In other words, the provisional application may not have any value if you are going to do a lot more work on your idea in the interim. You will need to file new provisional applications if you make notable changes, additions, or improvements to your invention.

Filing a provisional patent application for the Burpee Baby Bottle would allow for more time to develop the product and its processes. This sets your priority date for the product but gives you more time to draft the formal patent application.

Regular patent applications (provisional and nonprovisional)

The **patent application form** will require you to provide:

> ➤ A written summary or abstract describing your invention and its purpose. With the Burpee Baby Bottle, you would describe the invention as a baby bottle that has an air-releasing mechanism to help eliminate air that passes on to the baby.

> ➤ A graphic representation of your invention and its parts (a drawing or sketch). For the Burpee Baby Bottle, you would likely include a sketch of the bottle along with description about the different parts/ aspects of the air-releasing mechanism.

➢ A specific category under which your invention falls, including options such as acoustics, buckles, and ships, among hundreds of others. The USPTO has a list of invention categories in its Manual of Classifications (**www.uspto.gov/web/offices/opc/documents/caa.pdf**).

➢ Background or history on the category of your invention, which states the need for your invention and how it improves on the status quo. For the Burpee Baby Bottle, you would include background on baby bottles, describing the need for burping a baby every ten or so minutes and how using regular bottles without burping the baby will lead to the baby spitting up or getting stomach aches. Then explain how your Burpee Baby Bottle design will overcome these problems.

➢ A narrative description of the drawing.

➢ A detailed narrative description of all the materials, components, processes, and sequence of events ideally involved in using your invention.

The application has three main sections: the claims, the specifications, and the bibliographic. The claims are the part of the application a court will examine if you accuse someone of infringing on your patent. The specifications talk about the details of the invention, what it is made of, and how it works. They create the protective barrier that separates your invention from your competition's product. A patent attorney should draft claims to give you the full coverage available by law. The bibliographic section provides identifying information such as dates and serial numbers.

The claims outline what it is you have a monopoly on. However, the broader your claims, the narrower your monopoly. This may seem counterintuitive because the patent is supposed to prevent a competitor from doing all the things listed in your approved claims section. They can do some of it without infringing, but they cannot do all of it. But your claims are a package deal. The more specific elements in that package, the more likely a competitor can achieve the same outcome while skipping a step. That is all a competitor needs to circumvent your patent and your monopoly. For example, if you say your invention is "a piece of cotton glued to a 2-by-4," a competitor could easily nail a piece of cotton to a different sized piece of wood and call it his or her own. However, if you had written your invention is "a piece of cotton attached to a piece of wood," it is now harder to circumvent those specifications.

The claims are a highly critical and technical aspect of the patent application. Weakly constructed claims may lead to an approved application, but competitors will circumvent it easily. If that happens, you will have spent time and money but gained no significant intellectual property protection.

The specifications should provide enough information for a person of average skill in your field to use the invention reasonably easily. They also should describe what you believe to be the ideal way of using the invention. Both of these components are required in order for the examiner to approve your patent application. Be clear in your description, but remember the more detail you disclose in this area, the more you inform potential competitors about your design. A lot of detail can help designers find a way to design around your claims and obtain the same results without paying you a royalty. Take care to only include what is legally required and nothing more.

Foreign applications

Foreign patent applications will require an attorney's assistance, but you still should know how to prepare for the process. U.S. patents protect your intellectual property only in the United States. To obtain protection elsewhere, you will need to apply for foreign patents. A note of advice: In order to master a foreign patent, master a domestic one first. The U.S. General Accounting Office advises this because the benefits rarely outweigh the total costs of obtaining a foreign patent. Also, if there is a domestic one in place, this prevents competition from getting a hold of information and manufacturing in the United States before you, the original inventor, can do so.

Many countries' governments are signatories to international intellectual property treaties and conventions that govern filing procedures for foreigners. The International Convention for the Protection of Industrial Property, known as the Paris Convention, is an international treaty governing reciprocal patent filing rights among industrialized nations. If you are a patent applicant in any member nation, the treaty entitles you to file a corresponding patent application in other member countries within a year of the earliest filing date. It is one of the largest treaties in the world, involving 173 out of the 195 nations — including Vatican City, Kosovo, and Taiwan — in the world. Other treaties offer the same type of reciprocal rights to member countries, but the treaty that offers the best international protection is the Paris Convention.

Obtaining foreign patents is expensive, about $6,000 minimum, and complicated. It is worth pursuing a foreign patent only if you are certain a large market exists in the countries where you are applying, if you have a foreign licensee lined up, or if a licensee is paying for the patent application. According to patent attorney David Pressman in his book *Patent It Yourself,* "Filing [for a patent] in the United States usually gives you ten to 50 times more bang for your buck than filing abroad, which costs ten to 50 times as much anyway."

If you are interested in foreign patent protection, one option is to file applications in the desired nations all at the same time. This idea of having to file a single patent application in each country really shocks some inventors. An easier way, however, is to file through the Patent Cooperation Treaty (PCT). This agreement gives inventors protection in 147 nations, which are all part of the Paris Convention, associated with the treaty through a simple process. The clock starts on a PCT application once a U.S. application is filed. Many inventors have not heard of a PCT or simply think it is a foreign patent and know nothing of this process. Educate yourself on PCTs before filing; the USPTO website has extensive information on these applications.

Patent Attorneys and Agents

Many inventors use patent attorneys or patent agents to fill out and file patent applications. The USPTO does not require you to use an attorney, but inventors may turn to an attorney or agent because the process is complex and technical. These professionals may make the process less daunting.

Two types of professionals can help you obtain a patent: patent agents and patent attorneys. A **patent agent** is registered with the USPTO to represent inventors in the patent application process. This person is knowledgeable, usually with a scientific and invention background, and has passed USPTO exams. Although not an attorney, a patent agent is certified to act in the place of a patent attorney. A **patent attorney** is a member of the bar, and most have degrees in the sciences or engineering. The main difference between the two is that agents cannot litigate in court or draw up contracts. Having a patent agent handle an application from start to finish typically costs from $2,000 to $5,000, and a patent attorney would cost about $4,000 to $10,000. Even if you believe in the strength of your invention, make sure it is worth the expense.

The USPTO charges significant fees for the various stages of patent filing. *See the Appendix for the most common fees.* Patent attorneys charge anywhere from $100 to $500 per hour for the work they do for you. The trick is to find an attorney who charges a reasonable rate and can get the job done efficiently and with high quality. Remember, an attorney with experience and extensive knowledge of the patent application process may cost more, but he or she will provide you with a patent application that is properly completed. The best way to navigate this process is to interview several patent attorneys before selecting one.

When interviewing patent attorneys or agents, ask about their education — they should be intellectual property law specialists. Every agent or attorney should have his or her registration with the USPTO, the number of patent applications he or she has filed and obtained, and his or her experience with other aspects of intellectual property law, including other protections, such as copyright or trademarks, and other aspects of inventing, such as licensing or patent infringement actions. Also, make sure the attorney is willing to work with you and answer all of your questions. Neither of you will be happy if you do not work well together.

Although you may have little control over the cost of filing and the hourly rate of a good patent attorney, you do have some control over the amount of an attorney's time you require. The most complex aspects of the patent application are searching for prior art and drafting claims, but you can do this on your own. If you have time to work on the patent application and would rather spend your time than your money, your time will be well spent initiating the application process and doing as much of the groundwork as possible. Even if the attorney has to redo some of your work, you will have answered many of the questions the attorney would be asking you, and you may save the attorney time and yourself money.

CASE STUDY: ADVICE FROM AN IP ATTORNEY

Adam Philipp
Intellectual Property Attorney
AEON Law Group
www.aeonlaw.com

Adam Philipp is an intellectual property attorney practicing patent procurement, patent portfolio management, intellectual property strategy and planning, intellectual property licensing, and technology law with AEON Law Group. AEON is an intellectual property, technology, entertainment, and litigation law firm. Philipp has been involved in the prosecution of patent applications in computer sciences, electrical devices, and related fields since 1998 and with Internet and technology -related law since 1995. He also counsels clients on patent portfolio strategy, patentability, and infringement matters. His area of emphasis covers a wide variety of patent, trademark, and trade secret issues. Philipp is admitted to practice patent law with the U.S. Patent and Trademark Office.

SELECTING A PATENT ATTORNEY

According to Philipp, "Inventors don't just need an IP attorney; they need a patent attorney or a patent agent. If they haven't passed the patent bar, they're not allowed to file documents on your behalf at the patent office. If they're not regularly doing that, then odds are they aren't the best person to be giving you advice on the matter."

Some IP law firms provide free initial consultants or meetings. These typically do not include legal advice, but they can include pointers and good practices that apply generally to inventors. "Even if inventors pay for one hour of advice, that's often worth it because it can help set the inventors' strategies and let inventors know when their schedules and deadlines are," Philipp said. "They can then run the businesses without this question hanging over them about whether they should pursue patents now."

The foremost criteria for selecting a patent attorney is finding somebody the inventor can communicate well with. "The patent attorney translates your technical vision into a legally protecting document," he said. "If you don't communicate well, feel comfortable, or understand each other, choose another attorney."

Experience is critical in selecting a patent attorney for complex matters. Although law schools offer classes on intellectual property protection, they do not offer much practical experience. "The patent legal field is very much a guild system with masters, journeymen, and apprentices," Philipp said. "As with any other asset, patents have value, and the higher their potential value, the more worthwhile it is for the inventor to invest in having an experienced patent attorney maximize that value."

Philipp notes, "It's not hard to get a patent; it's hard to get a good patent. Getting a patent attorney with the experience to draft a patent application with the right scope is important. Patent attorneys have developed their processes to craft patent applications broad enough to give coverage but narrow enough to not infringe on prior art, and that skill comes with years of experience."

Some inventors will need attorneys with a background in the technical field of the invention. For example, some intellectual property attorneys have engineering, software, or science backgrounds that enable them to understand the technical jargon and claims involved with their clients' inventions. Philipp points out that though the attorneys at AEON specialize by technical field, "any one of us could work on a beach chair."

GETTING THE MOST VALUE FROM YOUR PATENT ATTORNEY RELATIONSHIP

Philipp counsels inventors to contact a patent attorney as soon as they have a firm idea for a product, especially if it is their first invention. "Inventors don't need to start spending money or get involved in big projects right away," he said, "but for somebody who's never been involved in the process, they can get some very good pointers about what not to do that will be potentially much more valuable than the substantive work they will pay for later."

The patent attorney's job is to provide legal advice. They may provide inventors with introductions to people who do industrial design, manufacturing, or finance if need be, but their expensive time is best used for the precise tasks for which they are trained: helping the inventor develop and pursue his or her IP strategy.

In Philipp's opinion, "A bad use of IP attorneys would be for them to seek licensing deals for you. That's outside their normal area of expertise and very expensive. It would be the role of an IP attorney to be involved in creating license agreements for the inventor or reviewing proposed licenses from the licensee." Patent attorneys do not typically involve themselves in commercialization strategy or other business decisions, "other than advising on how patent schedules work."

For patent attorneys to be effective, inventors cannot be either too intimidated or too cheap to talk with them as necessary. Some clients do not want to look bad in front of their attorneys, so they do not ask questions that could lead to greater mutual understanding of the inventors' goals. Other inventors want to avoid communications for which they will be billed. Working out a flat fee for particular services can set an inventor's mind at ease about calling or e-mailing the attorney when a question or new information arises. The patent attorney's job is to protect the inventor, and he or she can only do that effectively if the inventor talks.

When attorneys "don't have enough information or they get bad information, it's not going to help the inventor," notes Philipp. "All the disappointments that I can recall have stemmed from inadequate communication between the inventor and the patent attorney. Most attorneys are not there trying to suck fees out of the client. It may seem like it because many charge by the hour and it adds up fast. They are trying to meet the needs of the client, and they're going to make their best judgment about what those needs are."

PATENT STRATEGY

Philipp views patents as "business tools." It is the attorney's job to create those tools, but decisions about how to use them are up to the inventor. Philipp provides an example of an inventor with "technology might both apply horizontally across the marketplace or, with modifications, be enhanced very specifically to apply to a **vertical market.** In the vertical market, let's say the licenses are $10,000 per product, but maybe you only sell 100. In the **horizontal marketplace,** maybe it's only $10 per product, but you sell 1 million." It is the inventor's job to decide which market is more attractive if the patent cannot cover both. The patent attorney participates in crafting the business tool based on the inventor's decision about which direction to go.

"Some of my most devoted clients are ones whom I've told don't bother, or this isn't good enough, go back to the drawing board and come up with something new," says Philipp. "I routinely share my opinions about whether it's worth pursuing and whether it is patentable. If a patent won't make you more money than it costs to get it, think long and hard about whether you want to have it."

There are many business choices that can be made around IP issues, and they are best made with full information and professional advice. Philipp says, for example, that the United States offers a one-year grace period between disclosure and patent application deadline, but other countries do not. An inventor interested only in protections in the United States who is short on cash and wants to spend his or her capital on marketing might do well to wait before applying for a patent. This can be a sound business decision as long as the inventor makes it as part of a larger business strategy and in full knowledge of its potential implications.

USING YOUR PROTECTION

"One of the most valuable things you get with a patent," said Philipp, "is you create fear, uncertainty, and doubt with your competitors. Now they have to think long and hard if they want to enter that marketplace." Some advice books discourage inventors from pursuing patents because of the cost of enforcing them, but "there are contingent fee patent litigation attorneys, so you don't always have to be rich to enforce a patent," he said. "The only people who can safely infringe are those with no money. If you have no money and you're infringing on a solo inventor, you may have nothing to lose now, but you'd better hope you don't get big."

According to Philipp, "A patent really does keep competitors out of the market. You can get them to reevaluate their positions. It might be an exit strategy, they may think you are small potatoes, but it's worth it for them to buy you out so you're not a thorn in their side — it doesn't have to be 'license or litigation,' it can be a lever to move bigger players."

A typical scenario where an inventor might seek the advice of a patent attorney could involve an inventor who wants to submit an idea to a company. "It's fairly standard policy with most large companies that they will not agree to any confidentiality or obligation for unsolicited ideas," Philipp said. "So the obligation is on the inventor to independently provide some type of wrapping of intellectual property around it. If it's a book being submitted, you have copyright. If it's a useful device, patents are the vehicles."

THE IP PORTFOLIO

Intellectual property does not consist of patents alone. A patent attorney can help inventors determine whether they would benefit from a package of IP protections such as a patent and a trademark or a patent and a copyright. "In software," Philipp notes, "it is very common to have copyright and patent working together. In the apparel and outdoor industries, with bags, you'll sometimes have design patents and copyright of the bag's pattern."

For example, "Say there is one competitor copying the key idea behind a backpack's patented internal load balancing system [the bag's metal frame], but they are putting a different bag on it. That is a utility patent infringement." On the other hand, "If someone bought one of your bags, cut out the seams, traced the patterns, and recreated your bag on an industrial scale, than that could be a design patent and a copyright infringement." Having the advice of a patent attorney can help inventors create the appropriate IP protection package for their invention.

*If you would like to learn more about Phillipp and his firm, AEON Law Group, visit the website at **www.aeonlaw.com**.*

The Patent Application Process

Many inventors consider a patent the most important measure of success in inventing; these are inventors who have not profited from their inventions. Getting your invention into the hands of consumers and making profits truly proves your success as an inventor. A patent is an important component of the intellectual property protection that distinguishes your invention from the fleeting inspiration of some other person. In effect, the patent allows you to monopolize the market for your invention. Such protection positions you to profit from your invention and prevent others from doing so.

In the United States, a patent is the time-limited right to stop others from making, using, or selling your invention. The federal government confers this right, and you can enforce it through lawsuits or threats of lawsuits. If a court finds that a person or organization has infringed on your patent rights, your awards may include monetary damages and injunctive relief, which is a court order to cease the infringement and pay a monetary penalty if infringement continues.

The first step in patenting your invention is filling out an application. If you are planning to file an application for a utility patent (because of the increased complexity with a utility patent), you will benefit from the work of a patent attorney to draft the claims section, but you can pull together all the information needed for the application and make the attorney's task simpler and quicker, which in turn saves you money.

As noted at the beginning of this chapter, there are several types of patents, and you may want to apply for one or more types depending on the unique features of your invention. Following is a breakdown of what should be included in applications for design and plant patents. *Design and plant patents are also discussed in the Appendix, and design patents are briefly discussed in Chapter 3.*

To apply for a design patent, you need to include the following sections in your application:

> **Preamble:** The name of the applicant, a description of the invention and what it will be used for.

> **Claim:** One claim about your design — the key aspect of it that covers the entire invention.

> **Sketches/pictures:** A drawing or sketch of your invention; this is the most crucial aspect of the application. You can also include a black and white photograph of your invention.

> **Declaration:** Your statement that you have the right to apply for the patent.

For a plant patent, you will need to include the following in your application:

> **Overview/description:** An explanation about the plant and what makes it unique from other plants (should be in botanical terms).

> **Origin:** An explanation of the plant's parents and the process by which you used to make the parent plants reproduce and form the new plant.

> **Botanical name:** The genus and species of the plant (in Latin).

> **Drawing:** An artistic drawing of a the plant, detailing the features and colors (needs to be in color).

> **Declaration/oath:** Your statement that you have the right to file the patent and also an oath that you asexually reproduced the plant.

Patent deadlines

Patent law is about being first and being unique. To prove you were first, establishing the timeline of your invention process is critical. Your inventor's notebook and signed witnesses' statements are your proof that you thought of the idea in question first. You also must show you have been engaged in reducing your invention to practice — proving it works by making a prototype.

The patent application process is deadline-driven. The first deadline you must be concerned with is the 12-month window of time between when an idea enters the public domain and when you must file a patent application.

Your idea enters the public domain when:

➢ You tell someone about your invention without restricting his or her ability to share the information through a nondisclosure agreement.

➢ You disclose information about your invention with the intention of selling or licensing the invention.

➢ You or anyone else publishes a document with information about the invention, including a provisional patent application, brochure, academic paper, or magazine article.

The safest way to make sure your invention has full intellectual property protection is to file a full utility patent application at the earliest possible date, after you have researched enough to know that a similar patent that might exclude yours does not exist. Also, this is only if you decide that a patent is definitely the way to go, which may not always be the case.

After you have filed a patent application, the next deadline is filing an information disclosure revealing any prior art your research has identified. You have a legal duty to turn over any prior art you think might influence a patent examiner's decision. You may have already done this in your initial patent application. If not, you have three months to get it done. Finally, you have one year after filing a patent application in which to file for foreign patents. If your patent is approved, the USPTO will require you to pay regular maintenance fees at 3.5, 7.5, and 11.5 years.

Hearing back from the USPTO

Shortly after you submit your application, you will receive either an electronic confirmation if you filed through the USPTO website or a postcard confirmation if you filed through the mail. In order to receive a postcard from the USPTO, you need to provide a self-addressed postcard with your application. Note that getting a postcard confirmation could take up to a month. The confirmation is an acknowledgement that your application has been filed and should contain a serial number or application number. Keep this number confidential. Now, your patent is pending. A few months later, you will receive a receipt with more detailed information, including the examining group that will review your application. This receipt is an acknowledgement of the particulars of your application, confirming that the USPTO has created a file on your application and has begun evaluating it.

Anywhere from six to 24 months later, you will get a status report from the USPTO. The time depends on many factors, including the type of patent and how busy the office is. You will receive an official letter, or First Office Action (OA). This form and letter will come from the examiner reviewing your application. It is possible, but unlikely, that the OA will tell you your application is approved. More likely, the letter will include a list of problems the examiner found on your application. These could be rejections because prior art has been discovered that makes your invention not novel or obvious (to someone of average skill in your field who has read all the prior art), or the rejection could be based on problems in your specifications or claims. This is not the end of the process.

You will have several months in which to respond to the examiner's findings. When you respond to the examiner's findings, it is useful to turn to the services of a patent attorney. Then, several months after you submit your response, you will hear back from the examiner with the "final" finding. The timeline will change depending upon how much time the patent attorney has to devote to your case. If your patent application is rejected after you have responded to the examiner's findings, you have a few options. You may reply to the examiner either to state your reasoning why you think you are right and the examiner is wrong, request a third round of back-and-forth with the examiner (called a continuing examination), change your claims in the way the examiner suggested, or narrow your claims, which reduces your patent's value. You also can file a continuation application, which is a new application that retains the original filing date of the first application but is submitted for a modified form of your invention. You can, of course, also abandon your patent application. If you abandon the application, you may then pursue other forms of intellectual property protection available to you and continue efforts to license or build a business around your invention. These other protections are discussed in the coming chapters.

If your application is accepted, you must pay a fee for your patent to be issued and submit formal drawings of your invention if you have not already done so. You will be notified of the date when your patent will be issued and, shortly after that date, you should receive a letter or deed confirming your patent from the USPTO.

Maintaining your patent

If your patent is awarded, you will have to pay an issuance fee to get the USPTO to issue it. The patent may make you feel like a real inventor, but remember: Its purpose is to protect your monopoly from infringement by others. To maximize this protection, decide whether you want to mark your patent number on the products made under the patent; such marking enables judges to award you damages from parties found guilty of infringing on your patent, but it also provides a roadmap for competitors who want to design around your patent. If you have created a highly lucrative item, you can expect competitors to make enormous efforts to get in on the action. In that case, not marking your product may provide a deterrent to their finding and reading your patent description and drawing. However, your patent can still be found and read on the USPTO website, so not marking could also not benefit you. It is your call whether you would rather be positioned to collect damages — remember, suing is expensive — or keep a higher hurdle for competitors to jump over in finding your description and sketch.

Advantages of creating your own drawings

Patents will require patent drawings. There are several major advantages of creating your own patent drawings. One of the most obvious is cost, but equally important are the time considerations and the security of your invention.

An average patent drawing should cost between $100 and $200. In some instances, especially with complex exploded drawings, the cost can be higher. Because there are few patents that could be successfully submitted with a single drawing, this cost often runs into the thousands of dollars.

One caution must be added at this point: If you are seeking quality, beware of some Internet advertisers who claim to produce professional patent drawings. There are companies online that advertise patent drawings for less than $30 each. If you pay $30 for a drawing, do not expect a $200 drawing. The quality may be significantly less than what is considered acceptable by the USPTO. If the USPTO does not accept the drawings and requires a resubmission, you may have no recourse with these vendors. In addition, you will have to arrange for new drawings, on the USPTO's schedule. This can get costly, as you will now be paying premium for a quick turnaround. The premium paid to have the drawings created on your schedule can often double the price. In some instances, companies will allow customers to "buy the shop," or use all their available resources until the drawings are complete. This is a very costly option, but it may be the only available option to meet the USPTO's schedule. For the quality that is required, you will rarely find bargains.

As you can gather from that caution, there is a right way and a wrong way to create patent drawings. Remember, regardless of how great your invention is and how well it works, without a patent to protect it, you are giving the rights to produce the invention to anyone who wants to copy it. Filing a patent disclosure with the proper drawings and illustrations will protect your time and effort. Creating the drawings yourself will help in assuring the security of your invention.

The subject of time has already been mentioned repeatedly. When filing a patent, time is of the essence. The sooner the patent is filed, the sooner the inventor is protected. It is the first patent for an idea that is awarded. Therefore, the sooner the patent disclosure can be filed, the higher the likelihood of the patent being granted.

When you are using third parties to create the drawings, you are on their schedules. Your work is performed on the basis of their workloads. You can pay premiums to help meet your goal, but these are often costly. That is an obvious time factor, but there is a time factor that is less obvious. Although you are familiar with your invention, the people who will be creating the drawings are not. You will need to allow adequate time to explain the drawing to them. Often, the time required to explain the invention far exceeds the time required to make the physical drawings. When you consider these points, you can see why it may be quicker to create your own drawings.

Then there is the issue of security. Security is important to your patent. There are companies that survive on stealing other people's ideas. Many of these drafting or commercial drawing firms advertise regularly in magazines and on the Internet. They offer patent services and financial assistance to the inventor. In reality, they are seeking new products that can be profitable, and they will make sure they manage to patent them first. This happens quite frequently, especially when dealing with offshore companies and agencies.

That is not to say all companies offering assistance intend to steal your product. However, when it comes to a new invention, the best security is to discuss the invention with no one, at least until the patent application has been filed. This applies not only to those wishing to help you, but also those to whom you turn for help. There are a number of contract manufacturers, most offshore, that can have your product on the market quickly — but only after they have produced and patented it in their own country. In working with a third party to create patent drawings, or for any other reason, you have lost much of your security and may reduce the success of gaining a patent.

Thus, there are three reasons why the reader should consider creating his or her own patent drawings:

1. There can be substantial cost savings.

2. Having the drawings done by third parties puts you on their time schedules, not the other way around.

3. Creating your own drawings maintains the security for your invention.

These should be reason enough for the reader to tackle the task; however, there is a fourth reason just as compelling — your personal satisfaction. This is the satisfaction you gain from completing the job without the assistance of others. By creating your own drawings, they become another facet of your invention.

Here are some example drawings to help you get an idea of what you need to provide:

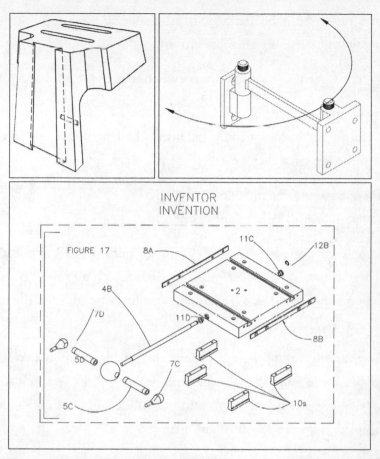

ABOVE PHOTOS REPRINTED FROM *HOW TO MAKE YOUR OWN PATENT DRAWINGS AND SAVE THOUSANDS: EVERYTHING YOU NEED TO KNOW EXPLAINED SIMPLY* BY ATLANTIC PUBLISHING AUTHOR JACK KOLLER

Publish (and Perish?)

The USPTO will publish your patent application within 18 months of its submittal. It may take another 18 months, however, before you receive a patent, if one is awarded. Having your patent application published has a variety of drawbacks:

> ➤ Between publication and award of the patent, a competitor can read your application and start trying to circumvent your claims in an

effort to capture the market with a competing product before you are able to manufacture your invention.

➢ Patent applicants have to pay a fee when their application is published.

➢ Publication lets people who may be aware of prior art or competitors who do not want your idea patented challenge your application by submitting what they believe to be prior art.

➢ If your application includes trade secrets, they will no longer be secret and will lose all rights to protection.

Patent applicants can ask the USPTO not to publish their application by submitting a nonpublication request (NPR). Given all the drawbacks to publication, why would anyone want an application published? Here are a couple reasons:

➢ If your invention's patent claims are infringed upon between the publication date and the patent award — this period is called **pendency**, when your application is public and pending — you can still claim damages against an infringer.

➢ You can request that your NPR be revoked if you have one in place and later decide to file a foreign application, but unintentionally failing to revoke it can have serious consequences.

Action Steps

Determine if your invention is patentable — or should be patented. Think about your idea and answer the following questions:

➢ Is there already a patent for your product? If the answer is yes, then your idea is not patentable.

> Will your invention be profitable enough to justify the cost of obtaining and maintaining a patent? And when thinking about profits, remember to think about all of your costs. *This is discussed in more detail in Chapter 11.*

Determine how to complete the application process. Consider your application options.

> If you are going to enter the patenting process, which type of application do you need to submit? Are you able to pay for the services of a patent attorney or patent agent? Have you researched the process enough to submit without the help of an attorney or agent?

> Do you have all of the required parts of the application submitted without revealing all of your information for competitors to use?

> Will you need to submit a foreign patent application to protect your invention internationally?

> Should you have your application published or choose to fill out an NPR?

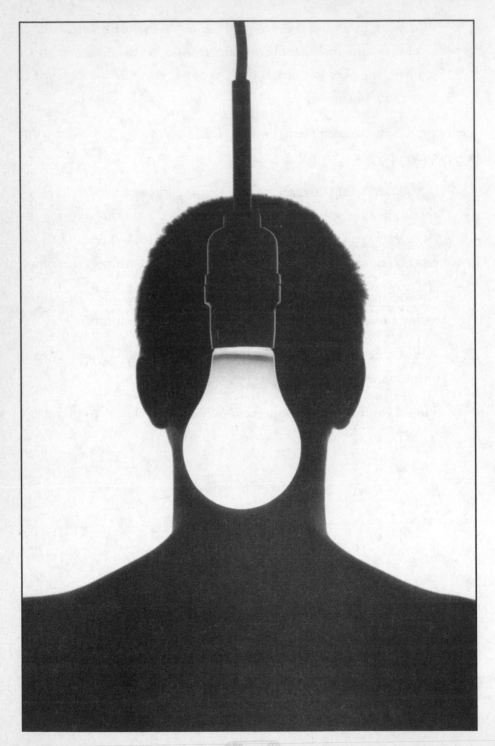

CHAPTER 5:

Other Intellectual Property Protections

"Invention, it must be humbly admitted, does not consist of creating out of void, but out of chaos."

— MARY WOLLSTONECRAFT SHELLEY,
AUTHOR OF *FRANKENSTEIN*

Besides patents, there are other ways of obtaining intellectual property protection. One simple thing every inventor can and should do is to keep a detailed, dated, and witnessed notebook. Two similar ideas include keeping an inventor's notebook, an inventor-signed and dated documentation of each step of the inventor's thought process, and writing a witnessed statement, a witness-signed and dated document describing the invention's features and attesting to the witness's understanding of those features. Some other non-patent options are detailed in this chapter.

Trademarks

A **trademark** is a word, symbol, phrase, sound, or smell that represents a product to the public. Many trademarked logos and symbols are widely recognized, such as McDonald's golden arches, the Pepsi™ logo, and the MasterCard® logo. Examples of trademarked sounds are the chimes for TV broadcaster NBC and the Yahoo! Yodel. Perfume scents are examples of trademarked smells. Your brand name, logo, or other symbol(s) differentiate your product from a competitor's.

To be protected, the trademark must either be used in commerce or registered with the USPTO with the intent to use it. Although use in commerce is sufficient to establish trademark rights, registration can strengthen trademark enforcement efforts. It is important to use trademarks to protect your brand name from infringement. A trademark can add significant value to your brand.

Symbols

The letters TM in superscript next to a word, brand, or logo used in commerce is sufficient to designate that the word, brand, or logo is trademarked. The ™ designates a nonregistered trademark. A trademark that has been registered with the USPTO is designated with the ® symbol. Use of the ® for a nonregistered trademark could interfere with your right to register it later. Registering a trademark offers you protection if another company uses the same name because it establishes your ownership of the name.

Commercial identifiers

A trademark is a **commercial identifier** — something that links your company and its products with some association in the minds of consumers.

Trademarks are protected because they are often tied to a company's reputation. A company that works hard to build a positive reputation and has their reputation associated with a particular mark would be negatively impacted financially if someone with a lesser-quality product appropriated that mark and the goodwill that goes with it.

There are several types of marks or commercial identifiers. Some identify products or brands and are called trademarks. Others identify services: service marks, certification marks, and association marks. Still others identify companies and are known as trade names. Legal protection even extends to distinctive and recognizable packaging that consumers automatically associate with a particular brand. The use of distinctive colors, shapes, and ornaments on packaging, uniforms, buildings, trucks, and other objects is known as trade dress. If you wanted to put syrup in a bottle shaped like a lady in a skirt with a bandana on her head, you would have trouble because Mrs. Butterworth's® syrup already has that registered.

Brand identity and brand equity

Some brands are defined by their commercial identifiers. What do you think of when you see a delivery person in brown slacks and shirt? UPS. What do you think of when you see a checkmark on athletic clothes? Nike.

The mark itself takes on value as a company establishes its reputation. For example, think about the Olympic rings logo. They appear on all sorts of products licensed by the International Olympic Committee. Consumers relate top athleticism, sportsmanship, and worldwide unity with these rings. A company would pay to associate themselves with the Olympic mark to capitalize on the value of the symbol to consumers and the goodwill it brings up in consumers' minds. **Brand identity**, which is the instant recognition of your logo and a positive association with your product, is an enormous marketing tool, one that you should build up and protect.

Companies with strong brand identities have what is called brand equity. They exploit and profit from trademarks in several ways. Coca-Cola® is a good example. They draw business through goodwill — or at least familiarity. They can license out their mark or name in a form of endorsement, pure profit for them as long as no scandal is attached to the product. Companies can create merchandise related to their monopoly. For example, kids' movies sell merchandise and gifts in fast-food restaurant meals before the films even premiere. Companies with strong, positive brand equity can introduce new products more easily. They can create a **franchise or turnkey operation** under the company or brand name that others purchase the rights to operate, which means they own that particular property and are responsible for its trademark protection and proper use. Trademarking your brand can keep competitors from benefiting from the goodwill you have generated through imitation of your mark, name, or dress.

Trademark protection

To be protected, the mark must either be used in trade or registered with the intent to use it. Although use in commerce is sufficient to establish trademark rights, registration with the USPTO can strengthen your enforcement efforts. Because there is no test or evaluation for a trademark other than its use in commerce, you will not know for sure the strength of your claim on your mark unless it is tested in court.

The criterion for evaluating this strength is **distinctiveness**, or originality. If there is no way anyone could confuse your scary FrankenBear with the cuddly teddy bears produced and marketed by others or with other Halloween toys and take-offs on the Frankenstein character, your mark is distinctive. If your graphic artist has devised an effective logo that does not resemble the logo for any other known product, and certainly not a product in your industry — think of the Coca-Cola script — then it is distinctive.

The more generic the name of your product, brand, or company, the less distinctive it is. If the name of a type of beer includes the word "beer," it would not be distinctive and thus not a protectable mark. It may be harder to be in business with a completely arbitrary mark. Somewhere in the middle is the suggestive mark, which nudges the consumer's unconscious with linkages and relationships that are not overtly obvious. Recipe website names are a good illustration of the range of protection of trade names. Recipe.com, RecipeSource.com, and AllRecipes.com tend toward the descriptive end of the scale, whereas Recipezaar.com tends more toward the suggestive, as it suggests a bazaar where recipes can be bought and traded. Yumyum.com indicates the simple joy your taste buds will experience with its recipes. Clever, cute, or funny names are often more memorable than easy names, but they are sometimes harder to remember. Try to imagine your main client base. Are they trendy, young, or old? Pick the name best suited to your product for your clients.

If your mark is not protectable because it is generic or if it may merit only weak protection because it is solely descriptive, you might not want to bother searching to see whether anyone else is using it. You likely could not prevail in suing them for infringement, and they likely could not prevail in suing you. If you think your mark is distinctive, make sure no one else is using it in the United States, or at least in your service area, before putting it into use.

There are some things a mark cannot do. A mark cannot be a generic term. For example, you cannot trademark the name "lipstick" for lipstick or "rock" for a rock you plan to sell, but you could brand your lipstick with the name "rock" and your rock with the name "lipstick." A mark also cannot be just your last name, and it cannot use deception, include swear words or pornography, replicate the insignia of another party, include a put-down of other people or organizations, or use a person's image without his or her permission.

Some marks that would be ineligible for protection when first put into use can become eligible for protection if consumers start to recognize them in association with your product. For example, hypothetically, a mark for Smith Brothers Farm™ milk may have little claim to protection when it first hits the market, but it may gain protection over time as its customers associate the qualities of the product with the mark. Marks that are initially entitled to protection also can lose that status if the name becomes too generic and if you do not actively protect the trademark. "Escalator" is an example of a once-trademark turned generic.

Prior mark searching

Just as a patent cannot be issued if the invention infringes on an already protected product, a trademark cannot be registered and will not have legal protection in court if it is not unique. Although you know enough not to use UPS or Nike as your brand name, who knows if there is already a Burpee Baby Bottle out there on the market? The only way to find out is to search for the product name.

Many trademarks are not registered because being in use protects them. That means you cannot search a central database for an authoritative conclusion that your mark does or does not infringe on someone else's. You can search other databases, including the USPTO's registry, your secretary of state's database, and industry trade association databases, but not finding your mark in these places does not mean someone else is not using it. Because these resources are incomplete, begin with the most complete resource available: the Internet. If you are using a made-up word, it should be simple to determine through an Internet search whether that term is in use. If you are using a real word, you will have to click and scan through many links, but it is doable. If you cannot wade through all the links that come up when you query a real word, use that word and the name of your industry.

If, after doing an Internet search, you do not find your mark in use, also search the USPTO register. The USPTO offers intent-to-use registration of marks that parties plan to use within the next six months. Intent-to-use registration can allow people or companies to establish priority, in effect reserving a mark even though it is not in use yet. The USPTO database provides access to these marks. Also, if you are challenged in court and have not even looked in the USPTO database, the judge may not look favorably on your case.

Trademark searches can be done professionally for between $300 and $1,200. Nevertheless, you can avoid these charges by using the Internet. Search registered and pending trademarks at the USPTO website **(www. uspto.gov)** and use the Trademark Electronic Search System (TESS). Go to the New User Form Search, type in the name you want to use, and click "Search Term." Be certain the "Field" term is on "Combined Word Mark." To make sure your search is comprehensive, be certain to perform the following:

> ➤ Enter all phonetically similar names of your company because names that are phonetically similar can cause conflicts in trademark use. For example, if you want to name your company Netflicks, you should enter Netflix as well.

> ➤ Enter the singular and the plural of your company's proposed name.

➢ If your proposed name has more than one word, enter each word separately.

➢ Use "wild card" search terms, such as the asterisk (*), to broaden your search. For example, if you are searching for Netflicks, you can enter Netfli* to search for similar names that began with the same six letters.

Be advised that trademark searches are not foolproof. Searches reveal only registered names. There may be unregistered business names in use as well. They would be considered valid even if they may not have shown up in the USPTO database. Consequently, after searching there, search the Internet for the proposed name. This would probably reveal any current users of your proposed name. If you have reached this stage without discovering any conflicting trademarks or service marks, search the secretary of state's records for existing corporate names.

If your name passes the previous tests, you may want to reserve it. This step is not absolutely necessary but is recommended as you move the planning and development stages of your new business. Most states offer a reservation service where you file a short name reservation form with the secretary of state, but there is a fee for this service that will vary with each state. When you have finalized your name, make sure you have a corporate suffix to make the public aware of your limited liability protection if you have decided to incorporate your business. There really is no difference among the three except for preference, but make sure to stick with one name all the way through. Include:

➢ Corporation or Corp.

➢ Incorporated or Inc.

➢ Limited or Ltd.; in some states, this suffix can be confused with a "limited partnership" or "limited liability corporation."

If you are likely to do business primarily in one geographic region, you can search the secretary of state databases in that area.

If you do find your mark in use by someone else, you still may be able to use it. You will need legal advice on this, but ask yourself whether your product or business is likely to be confused with that of the original holder of the mark. If that company makes toilet plungers and you make airline landing gear, it is unlikely people would be confused. If you both make sleep aids, and you use the same script and color of logo and call yours SleepDreams instead of SweetDreams, you may be in trouble even though the names are not identical. Another example is the lingerie store Victoria's Secret, which sued an adult novelty store named Victor's Secret for trademark infringement. The courts decided in favor of Victoria's Secret, and Victor's Secret changed its name to Cathy's Little Secret (Victor's wife's name). Your good sense can guide you in this search, but when in doubt, ask a lawyer.

Registering your mark

You can register a trademark with the USPTO prior to use in commerce, thereby establishing priority for the mark if you plan to use it relatively soon. Initial registration is good for six months, and you can extend it (for a fee) for up to three years. If you do not use the trademark before the intent-to-use registration expires, the trademark is considered abandoned. It then becomes public and available for others to adopt.

Although your mark acquires legal protection as soon as you use it in commerce, and the strength of that protection is based on its distinctiveness, you can still gain additional protection by registering your mark. About a quarter of all marks used in business are registered. If you are developing an invention for commercialization but already came up with a perfect, catchy brand name, register the name with an intent-to-use trademark application that will protect your right to use the mark for six months and can be extended for up to three years.

The benefits of registration include:

> Providing patent attorneys and judges with more tools for enforcing protection of your mark.

> Making it easy for others who want to use a similar or identical mark to find it is in use.

> Having the ability to prohibit infringing Internet domain names.

> Giving judges the ability to levy additional monetary damages for mark infringement.

> Enabling judges to restrain infringing parties, which prevents them from using the mark while you await a ruling on your rights.

> Stopping the importation of foreign items that infringe on your mark.

When you apply to register your mark, you will specify the items on which your mark will be used and the industrial classifications these products fall into. You must pay a fee for each category in which you seek registration. Just like claims in a patent, your mark may have several elements, including a combination of words, punctuation, color, and images. When deciding what to register, examine each element independently to determine which is the strongest. Someone might copy part but not all of your mark. If you select the strongest element of your mark — the component likely to have the broadest legal protection — and register it, anyone who uses that component will be infringing. If a word itself rather than the style it is written in is the mark, it is called typed format. The way the word is written, either the script or the combination of upper- and lowercase letters, is called a stylized or design format. A logo is known as a graphic mark.

Trademark law can be as arcane and convoluted as patent law, and retaining an intellectual property attorney to review your application, if not write it for you, is advisable. Once you file an application to register your mark, the process of having the mark approved will take about 18 months, though the entire process can take several years depending on any legal issues that may arise. Several rounds of objections and responses may take place during trademark registration just as with a patent application. This is an important area in which to have legal advice.

Reasons why the USPTO's examiners may refuse registration for a mark include possibility of confusion with an existing mark and lack of distinctiveness; your mark could be just too generic. In this case, you can request the USPTO place your mark on the Supplemental Register; this is a list that protects your priority for the mark while you use it in trade and hope that, over time, it acquires distinctiveness through association with your product in consumers' minds. Placing a mark on the Supplemental Register is tantamount to admitting your mark is not protectable. The advantage of being placed on the Supplemental Register is you retain a chronological priority with the USPTO. However, you will not be able to make a good case in court that your mark has been infringed because it has been found to be too generic.

When your mark is granted preliminary approval, it enters a period in which others can challenge or object to its registration. If a company thinks your mark is infringing on its mark or if it is offended by your mark, the company may file an objection. This will trigger an appeal before a trademark board. To pursue registration, you will have to hire an attorney to argue your case. If your mark is refused registration, you can appeal the examiner's decision with an attorney's assistance. Once you register a trademark, you must use the registered trademark symbol. Without the notice of trademark, you still have legal protection to stop infringement on your mark, but judges may not be able to impose damages on the infringer. Although trademark protection lasts for as long as the mark is in use, USPTO registration lasts six years. To extend the registration period, apply for an extension by providing evidence and a sworn statement that your mark is still in use. After the first renewal, your mark will remain registered for ten years and must be renewed at subsequent ten-year intervals.

Trade Secrets

A **trade secret** is information about your invention you want to keep out of the hands of your competitors. This type of intellectual property protection is not registered with the USPTO. You do not have to pay any application fees, and you do not have to hire anyone to help. Examples include a particular process, such as your process of making fiberglass; a set of ingredients or a formula, such as KFC Corp.'s secret recipe; or a combination of process and formula. As long as you keep the information confidential by means of nondisclosure forms and avoidance of public disclosure, a trade secret is protected indefinitely unless someone reverse-engineers the ingredients, independently discovers the same process or set of ingredients, or a combination of the two.

This is an effective and inexpensive intellectual property right that is legally protected. If someone has signed a confidentiality contract and goes on to reveal your secrets, that person can be sued. Only reveal your trade secrets to those who need to know and can be trusted. If keeping something a secret is not a viable option, securing your intellectual property with another type of protection, such as a patent or trademark, is wise. For example, if you need to include a number of people/organizations/institutions in the planning, designing, manufacturing, and commercialization of your invention, then you might want to secure intellectual property protection instead of relying on trade secret protection. Apple® is infamous for keeping its new products under wraps until close to the release date. In the summer of 2010, the company ran into customer complaints about this when the iPhone® 4 was released. Customers wanted to buy cases to protect the expensive phone, but the cases could not be made quickly enough because the companies that make the protective cases did not have the phone dimensions until they were released to the public. Case sales were backed up, and Apple ended up giving each iPhone 4 owner a free Bumper or other case as long as the owner bought the phone before September 2010.

Trade secret vs. patent

Patents can cover many inventions that trade-secret protections also can cover. To decide which intellectual property right is better for your invention, consider the following advantages and disadvantages of trade secrets:

Advantages:

> Trade secrets do not expire like patents, so as long as your trade secret remains secret, you remain protected.

> The cost of obtaining a patent can add up, but trade secrets have no formal cost.

> Trade-secret protection is instant protection.

Disadvantages:

> People can figure out your trade secret through research, such as reverse-engineering.

> Someone who concurrently develops by coincidence the same formula or process as you have can obtain a patent.

Copyright

Copyright is another form of intellectual property protection. Copyright protects original written works, artwork, music, and computer software. Written works that might be included with your invention include instructions and brochures. As with trade secrets, the government does not grant copyrights. Copyright protection takes effect as soon as a work is created and is the property of the person who created the work. No application or expense is necessary to get your work protected.

The symbol for copyright is ©, and you can attach it to any of your written materials associated with your invention. Some aspects of your invention might not be protected by copyright. For example, clothing designs are not protected. Instead, designers must apply for a design patent. Fonts also are not protected. In addition, unsubstantial works (e.g., titles, phrases, slogans, and common symbols) are not protected. These unsubstantial works may qualify for trademark protection, however.

For works created after Jan. 1, 1978, a work by a known author is covered by copyright during the author's lifetime, plus 70 years after his or her death. For works with two or more authors, the copyright extends for 70 years after the last surviving author's death. For a work with one or more anonymous authors, protection is the shorter of 120 years from creation or 95 years from publication. Your copyrighted work can be used without your permission for "fair use," such as reviews of the work, news reporting, classroom use/teaching, and research.

Although you do not have to file an application to have copyright protection on your work, you can register copyrights with the United States Copyright Office. In 2009, the fee for electronically filing a registration was $35, or

$50 to $65 to file by paper, depending on the form used. Different forms are used for different works. *See the Appendix for copyright forms.*

Action Steps

Look back at the questions you answered in the action step in Chapter 4. Now think about your invention in terms of the other types of intellectual property protections, such as trademarks.

Does it make more sense for your invention to bypass the patent in favor of other intellectual property protection (or none)? Remember that the patent application will be published and other manufacturers may be able to get around your patent and make a similar product.

CASE STUDY: BOOGIE WIPES®

Julie Pickens
Mindee Doney
www.boogiewipes.com

Julie Pickens and Mindee Doney are mothers in Beaverton, Oregon, and were "tired of chasing their kids around to clean their little red chapped noses." Using dry tissues made their kids' noses worse, so they started searching for alternatives. Their market research did not turn up many options. They discovered pediatricians' No. 1 recommendation for treating runny noses was saline, or sodium chloride, and decided to build their invention off of this recommendation. Their invention, Boogie Wipes, are like wet tissues, made with saline and also vitamin E and aloe to help soothe chapped noses. They come in different, child-friendly scents including Fresh, Great Grape, and Magic Menthol.

INTELLECTUAL PROPERTY PROTECTION

To protect their invention, Pickens and Doney decided to start with a provisional patent application so they could make changes for the first year, then apply for a non-provisional patent at the end of that year. They say applying for a patent "is a lengthy process and takes some time and money to do it well." They recommend starting with trademark protection: "Brand recognition and being the pioneer in a category can be as powerful as a patent. It's the combination that really makes people millions. There are hundreds of sticky things to put on a cut that's bleeding, but they are all called band-aids, and the 1926 patent Earle Dickinson got for inventing it did not keep Johnson and Johnson and many other companies from making a fortune on it."

ADVICE FOR INVENTORS

Pickens and Doney say you must be confident in your idea: "Stay positive, make sure your idea is different enough to get people to change their habits and take a risk on your innovation." They also say everyone will try to offer you advice — whether you ask for it or not — so be sure to stick to what you believe is best. "Things won't go according to plan, but if you don't have one to guide you, you're at the mercy of everyone else's idea of what you should be doing, and you will be left 'along for the ride' in your own venture."

CHAPTER 6:

Designing Your Idea

"Necessity, the mother of invention."

— GEORGE FARQUHAR, IRISH POET

Now that you have decided through careful research what idea to pursue and have mapped out a strategy for protecting your idea, it is time to create a design. To do this, you need to have an idea of what the product will look like or be. Your idea should be practical and easily understood by a wide consumer audience.

Paint a mental picture of the product in your head. However, in order for that idea to become an invention, you will need to get it on paper. Drawing a sketch — no matter how rough — enables others to visualize it. It also will help you know what to expect from your idea, plan, or project. By getting your idea down on paper, you can clearly see your product's dimensions and variables. You also can begin to visualize what materials you will need to create your invention. It will even make you think about things you might not have considered, such as size, shape, and color. Moreover, you are creating a hard-copy illustration to send to the USPTO when you apply for a patent. When you send your drawing in, though, make it as clear a picture as possible. Sending them your roughest first sketch is not a good idea.

Designing Your Invention

Whether you are attempting to market an idea or an actual product, putting it on paper will give you the specifics for manufacturing it. Convey your idea in a written proposal that gives step-by-step instructions as to what your idea is about. The proposal should answer these questions:

- ➤ What will your idea achieve?
- ➤ What do you need to pull the idea together?
- ➤ Is it an idea for a product already in use, or is it something totally different?

Writing everything down allows you to break the idea up into sections you might not have thought of before. Come up with a one-sentence description of the product. Then list your product's features and how your product is unique and original. Narrowing down exactly what the product is will help you in the creative process. It also will help later on with sales and marketing because you will have a better idea of what your product is and does. It is much easier to market a product when you can fully explain it to potential customers.

Stages of the design process

A **design process** is a series of steps for designing followed by most professional designers. The steps depend on the product or service you want to create. In some cases, some steps may be irrelevant, useless, or sometimes ignored. This may be done for the purpose of saving cost and time, or the step may be unnecessary for that particular process or situation.

Stages in design include:

> Pre-production design

> Design during production

> Post-production design

> Redesign

Pre-production design

This is the most important part of the process. It is the first outlook and the first molding stage for the product or process. This contains the following steps:

1. **Design brief**: A statement of the goals of the design. For the Burpee Baby Bottle, the goal of the design is to eliminate air in the bottle through a mechanism. The design must be sleek, and the bottle cannot be cumbersome. Therefore, it must be lightweight.

2. **Research**: The investigation of look-alike design in the current field or related fields and solutions already available.

3. **Design specification**: The requirement of the product or service, or the requirement of the user, which has to be incorporated into the design.

4. **Problem discovery**: All problems in the design have to be overcome, the concept looked into, and the whole design solution documented.

5.   **Improvements:** Present the design to the team, note the feedback they give, and improve the design.

You may want to hire a designer to help during this stage. If sketching the designs for the product on your own is not an option, hire a freelance designer. You can search for a prototype designer online or in the phone book. Another option is to contact the engineering department at a local college or university to find faculty or students who can help you. Students typically will work for less money — or even nothing at all, if they can get some sort of research out of your project — but keep in mind they are not as experienced. The United Inventors Association (**www.uiausa.org**) is another source for finding designers.

If you do decide to hire an outside person to assist with the design or any stage of the production, lay out your expectations in a written contract or agreement. Come up with a detailed description of the work you need to have done. Designers will give you estimates based on that job description. Get these estimates in writing, even if you are seeking help from people you know. You will have to decide whether you want to pay on a per-hour basis or pay a lump sum for the entire project depending on your needs and your specific project. The designer also might have a preference. If you decide to work on a per-hour basis, get an estimate in writing of the number of hours the designer thinks it will take to complete the job.

Your contract with the designer should detail the services, rates, expectations, deadlines, and specifications for your project. Designers usually charge anywhere from $20 to $125 per hour for their services, depending on the designer's experience, specialty, and location, and the product itself. Once you select a designer, have that person sign a confidentiality or nondisclosure agreement (NDA) to protect yourself and your product. *See the Appendix for a sample NDA.*

Production

Design during production consists of two steps: development and testing. **Development** means constant improvement to the design during the design process, and **testing** means in-site testing for problems during production. This stage of design will be useful after the prototype is made. Issues that might not be observed in the paper-and-pencil sketches or schematic design could show up with a physical representation of your invention. The design of the product does not end with a prototype because development changes the original schematic design. Depending on the time you can devote to your invention, the size and scale of your invention, and other factors, this stage could take as little as a month or as long as a year.

Post-production design

This stage of design is after the product has been produced or manufactured. *For more information about manufacturing, see Chapter 9.* Feedback is necessary for further development of future designs. **Implementation** is the first step in post-production design. In implementation, the design is introduced to the environment. The next step is evaluation: the product should fit in the market, and it should serve its purpose. Suggestions and constructive criticism from trusted family, friends, and experts, who have all signed confidentiality agreements, should be welcomed for improvements of the design in the future.

Redesign

The final step in the design process, making corrections, can occur in any one or all of the stages of the design process. It can be repeated as often as possible, which includes corrections at any time before the start of production, during production, or after production. When the product is at fault or some correction has to be made, the first design is evaluated and redesigned to incorporate the current needs. Enlist the help of a family member or close friend, but do not forget to protect yourself and your idea.

Do-It-Yourself Design

If you decide to design your product yourself, begin with the vision in your head you first had when you thought up the idea. Your inventor's log should build off of that vision with a thorough description of your invention. In addition, you may already have precise drawings or sketches of your invention in your log. In each step of the path to creating your invention, the better and more specific your drawings, the easier it will be to make a useful product.

Using a sketchbook or simply white paper, draw the design for your invention in pencil. An important tip for this step: Do not let any artistic shortcomings discourage you. Think of this as your starting point, even if it is not perfect. You may do several of these pencil-and-paper sketches. If you want to get feedback from anyone at this point in the design, remember to have each person sign a confidentiality or nondisclosure agreement.

You want your invention to be as simple as possible while still serving the purpose you are designing it for. Ask yourself these questions about your design:

- ➤ Is the design as simple as it can be?
- ➤ Does the design have the least possible potential problems? This includes components and parts.
- ➤ Does your invention still serve the function you designed it for?

Identifying potential issues before your product is on the shelf will ensure a quality product — and save your reputation. Of course, you will not spot every potential problem on a piece of paper. Therefore, you will go through a few additional steps before you begin to manufacture your product.

Schematic design

From your pencil-and-paper sketches, you will be able to create a graphic design. If you know computer-aided designing (CAD), you can easily create a graphic representation on your own; this is called a **schematic design**. In the schematic design, you will illustrate not only the product itself, but also the individual components of the invention and how they relate. Possibly unlike previous representations of the invention, the schematic design is always drawn to scale. It also includes specific information about the dimensions.

The most frequently used CAD program is Autodesk® Inventor™, 3-D design software. According to the Autodesk website (**http://usa. autodesk.com**), the manufacturer's suggested retail price for this software ranges from $3,995 to $4,425. Google SketchUp is a more cost-effective alternative, with a free version and a professional version for $495. According to its website (**http://sketchup.google.com**), Google SketchUp is "a software that you can use to create, modify, and share 3-D models."

Materials and processes

After you have decided on the major structure of your invention, the next step is to figure out what it will be made of. You might have already researched possible materials; if not, this is the time to put some thought into it. Check out similar products; experiment with different consistencies, textures, and colors; and pick an acceptable price point to find the best material for you. Describe the materials you choose, as well as techniques for building your product. If the invention has intricate parts, divide the information according to the different sections of the product. For example, the Burpee Baby Bottle needs to be portable so it needs to be lightweight. Most bottles are made of a lightweight, hard plastic strong enough to be durable. It also needs to be able to be washed and preferably dishwasher safe. The air-releasing mechanism also needs to be simple and lightweight. It needs to be liquid-proof or encased in something liquid-proof.

Again, you will want to write this information so anyone can understand what you are talking about. Think of it as simplified instructions on how to build your invention. If your invention does several different things, list each of the applications separately. When the product is manufactured, knowing the intentions for its use is crucial, and this step will make it much easier. At this stage, only be concerned with getting your idea down on paper or designing it so others can easily understand your intentions. What might seem perfectly fine to you when it is in your head might look much different once you have a chance to map it out and see it on paper.

Managing Design Constraints

There are two types of constraints to consider in the design phase: negotiable and nonnegotiable. **Negotiable constraints** are variables you can change and manipulate. **Nonnegotiable constraints** are variables you cannot change or control. You will need to identify, classify, and select these constraints. This takes some time. You then will have to manipulate the design variables to satisfy the nonnegotiable constraints and optimize the negotiable constraints.

Consider the design of a chair. A chair should be able to support a certain weight. This is a nonnegotiable constraint. The cost of production may be another nonnegotiable constraint. On the other hand, the aesthetic qualities and materials used to build the chair are negotiable constraints because you have more leeway when making choices. The nonnegotiable constraints should not directly conflict with the design. If they do, you must redefine the constraints.

Poor designs crop up as a consequence of mismanaged constraints. For instance, in the video-game industry, a successful game must be fun and entertaining, and it should not bore people. This should be a nonnegotiable constraint, which means a game design that does not meet this condition is likely to be unprofitable.

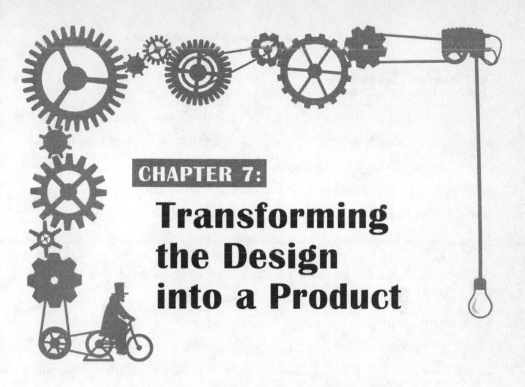

CHAPTER 7:

Transforming the Design into a Product

"Invention, strictly speaking, is little more than a new combination of those images which have been previously gathered and deposited in the memory; nothing can come of nothing."

— JOSHUA REYNOLDS, BRITISH PAINTER

At this point, you have thoroughly researched your product and refined your invention. You have kept an inventor's log of the process through which you have journeyed. You might have submitted a provisional application or full application for a patent. You have created a design from your vision of the product. You either have created a schematic design yourself or hired someone to do it for you. Now it is time to create a functional product.

The Prototype

The first step in making a physical rendering of your invention is the prototype. A working prototype will be useful at several points in the invention process and is a necessity for marketing and selling your invention. Your prototype is the first manifestation of your invention and is the basis for all future changes, so it is advantageous to start with a quality example.

Prototypes come in many forms, depending on what stage of the invention process you are in and the prototype's purpose. Keep in mind, too, that the reason for making a prototype is to work out kinks in the design. Therefore, your invention might go through a few — or even numerous — changes during the process. A working prototype model is not a legal necessity to obtain a patent for your invention; however, here are some ways your prototype will help you throughout the design and patent process:

> ➢ It will be one of the strongest ways you can establish yourself as the first inventor of the product.
> ➢ You can include the photos of prototypes in your invention logbook.
> ➢ It will help you identify design flaws of your invention.
> ➢ It will help you be certain about the exact size, shape, and form of the product.
> ➢ It will help you sell or license your invention.
> ➢ It will be useful during demonstrations and explanations for potential investors.
> ➢ It will help you write and make illustrations for the patent application.
> ➢ It will help you develop techniques for manufacturing the product on a large scale.

> It will help you calculate the cost per unit to manufacture the product.

Begin by making a nonworking model of your invention using wood, cardboard, metal, foam, or similar materials to test the product's size and form. Next, create a step-by-step procedure for making a working prototype. List all the materials and tools required to assemble it. At this point, you will need to decide whether you are capable of constructing the prototype on your own or whether you need to hire someone to do it for you. You may need some complex drawings if your invention is based on electronics. You also may need to refer to technical books or get help from qualified professionals. Whether you do it yourself or hire someone, making a working prototype can cost a large amount of money in some cases.

The Prototype Production Process

There are a few different types of prototypes, ranging from a crude prototype to the final prototype. Each step provides an opportunity to note potential problems, eliminate unnecessary components, and simply create a better final product.

The crude prototype

The **crude prototype** is your first attempt at making a sketch or schematic design into a physical product. It does not necessarily have to function the way you intend, but it does need to be a 3-D replica. You can use any material to make a crude prototype. It serves as a rough draft, so it does not need to be perfect. Construct your prototype without spending too much money. You can even use materials such as cardboard and duct tape. If you use cardboard, you can write notes on parts and draw pictures right on the prototype. You may need to build several crude models before you are ready to make a working prototype. Working out the kinks on cardboard is much more cost-effective than fixing problems later in the process. As you move along, you may want to create a crude prototype out of materials that better resemble the final product. You can buy these materials at a hardware or craft store, order them online, or even use materials from other products similar to yours. Keep detailed notes in your inventor's notebook about the process of creating a prototype.

The working prototype

When you are comfortable with the design of your crude prototype, the next step is to create the **working prototype** — or a prototype that functions. You can most likely build the crude prototype yourself; however, the working prototype may require assistance. First, decide what kinds of capabilities and processes your prototype will require. Different prototype makers specialize in different things. If your invention is a simple product or concept, consider trying to build it yourself. If your invention is a machine or something complicated, consider hiring someone. You can always try to make it yourself, and if you cannot get it right, then you can then hire someone. If you have an engineer friend or know someone who likes to (and can) build things, you might want to enlist that person's help. Your working prototype may need revisions as well. Keep revising until you have figured out the best and most cost-effective design for your invention. Remember to have anyone involved sign a confidentiality or nondisclosure agreement.

The final prototype

Like the name implies, your **final prototype** is the last prototype. This prototype will look and work like your manufactured product. It will be the model on which you will base your design for the assembly of your manufactured invention.

Do It Yourself or Hire a Professional?

The big decision in preparing your prototype is whether to make it yourself or hire someone to put it together for you. This can depend on many variables. Ask yourself a couple questions to determine the answer:

> ➤ **Are you equipped to build the model?** Although you may be able to put the information together in concept form and on paper, building the actual, working model may be a different story. If you have the expertise to build the prototype yourself, you can save the money it costs to pay a professional. Remember, this prototype is the example by which your hopefully commercialized product will be manufactured. Your representation of your invention needs to be sturdy and functional.

> ➤ **Do you have the resources to build the prototype?** You may spend more in materials, supplies, and tools than you would in hiring someone to build your model. Think about the necessary components of your invention and determine your access to the materials.

Using the Burpee Baby Bottle as an example, hiring a firm to build the prototype would be the only option if the inventor is new to the process and has no experience with design. The Burpee Baby Bottle would require materials and resources a new inventor would likely not be equipped with. Therefore, using this example, hiring a firm would be the smartest choice.

If you decide to make your own prototype, begin by writing a simple description of your invention, including a clear explanation of the materials used and how it works. Then, sketch and label a diagram that demonstrates the process. Even at this early stage, it may be helpful to contact a professional, such as an engineer or draftsman, to advise you. Break down these basic blueprints to identify the necessary parts for building your product. Researching mechanisms or similar technology may help you avoid some of the trial-and-error process involved in perfecting your prototype.

If you decide to seek help from a professional, consider the project. You may find an engineer, a designer, a manufacturer, or a professional prototype maker who can make your dream a reality. Although whom you choose will depend partially on the area you live in and who is available, much will also depend on your idea itself. Also, consider the amount of money you will need to build your prototype. Prototypes can be expensive, whether you are building it yourself or hiring a manufacturer. Cost is one of the biggest reasons to evaluate several different sources to make your prototype. Do not just settle for the first manufacturer who agrees to build it for you. Shop around and get quotes from different individuals or companies.

Similar to when you were searching for a potential designer for your idea, consider using the resources of a college or university in your area. Engineering departments might allow their students to work on your prototype as part of their teaching program. Depending on the idea you want to prototype, trade schools also may be a good place to look. If you would prefer a manufacturing company or professional prototype maker, you might want to start your search at the local library. Most libraries will have copies of trade directories that contain lists of manufacturers. You also can look in the phone book under "prototypes."

The Internet can also be a useful resource when looking for someone to manufacture your prototype. Try searching online for manufacturers who specialize in the specific area your idea falls into, i.e. electronics or household products. Another good resource is ThomasNet® (**www. thomasnet.com**), which lists products and services. Note, however, that this directory will not list small, one- or two-person manufacturers and machine shops.

In your search for someone to help you develop your prototype, you may find a manufacturer to help you develop your idea. The manufacturer may even give you helpful advice on the next steps in getting your idea on the market. Several organizations, including the Triton Foundation and the Industry Development Centre, can help you find manufacturers. Both of these organizations also can help you with market research and can even give advice on industrial designers.

If you hire someone to manufacture your prototype, you are not employing that person. Have a contract such as a work-for-hire agreement, along with a nondisclosure agreement. It is important to legally protect any information about your idea being made public by those you are trusting to produce your prototype. You need to protect your intellectual property at every step.

Prototype makers

> ➢ Alpha Prototype Makers (**www.alphaprototypes.com**): Alpha Prototype Makers specializes in fused deposition modeling services, "used to convert CAD drawings into physical parts;" stereolithography, which creates a 3D model with extreme detail; Polyjet, a machine that prints and builds parts, which, according to Alpha Prototype Makers, has "extremely high detail, fast build speed, and high-quality

parts" and is the "fastest growing segment of the rapid prototyping market place;" and urethane casting, a common plastic molding used for prototypes. According to the company website, prices are based on the turnaround time and material needed to build the product. For a single part up to 3 cubic inches, the cost is $149.

➢ Design Prototyping Technologies (**www.dpt-fast.com**): Design Prototyping Technologies is in Syracuse, New York. According to its website, "since 1993, DPT has been producing high-quality rapid prototypes for large and small companies." You can obtain a quote for services from DPT on the company website.

➢ T2 Design and Prototyping (**www.t2design.com**): Based out of Los Angeles, California, T2 Design and Prototyping was featured on ABC's show *American Inventor*. Some examples of design/prototypes created by T2 Design and Prototyping include Pepper-Mate Pepper Sprayer, Front Spoiler for Ford Explorer, Dispensa Filter, the Puppet Kooler, and the Piggybanker.

➢ Insight Prototype Model Makers (**www.prototypemodelmakers. com**): The company is based in Brewster, New York, and has been in operation since 1995. Some of their clients include Abercrombie and Fitch, Godiva Chocolatier, Cuisinart, and CNN. The company has many capabilities, including engraving, sculpting, welding, textile designs, tinting, color matching, and models.

Action Steps

Deciding whether you should make your own prototype of hire a professional is not a decision to take lightly. Your prototype could end up being the example you take to presentations. If you can put your prototype together with materials found at a hardware store — and it looks professional — you can save thousands of dollars in doing it yourself. However, if you prototype is more complex, you will want to find an expert to make your prototype.

If you decide to hire a prototype maker, research various ones. Decide what qualities are most important for your situation. For example:

> **Do you want someone local?** This can be convenient if you want to monitor the prototype making with regular meetings and inspections of the prototype. This not critical, but some people prefer being able to oversee the process. If the prototype maker is not in close proximity to you, be prepared to add some extra time for shipping of the prototype, as the manufacturer may send it to you at different stages of production for approval and feedback.

> **How much do you want to spend?** Find a balance between cost and quality. At this stage of the invention, you have made no money and still have no real guarantee that you will. On the other hand, as mentioned before, your prototype is an important step in the invention process and not something that should be thrown together.

> **Which of the prototype makers are most knowledgeable about the type of product you plan to have made?** Choosing a prototype maker with experience in the industry will save you time and possibly money. They will know the "way things are done" in your particular industry, and you have the added bonus of that extra experience.

CASE STUDY: BUBELE®
BABY CLOTHING

Kris Weisblatt
www.bubelebaby.com

In 2007, Kris Weisblatt gave birth to her youngest son. During the delivery, she suffered cardiac arrest, lost a lot of blood and oxygen, and was put into an induced coma. She was left with some minor brain damage but says she believes she is lucky to be alive. Weisblatt says when she was released from the hospital and returned home, she was thinking simplistically. Tired of pacifiers dropping to the floor, she thought of a simple fix: a loop sewn into the side seam of children's clothing and a "Snappy" that attaches to the pacifier and snaps around the loop.

DESIGN AND REDESIGN

Weisblatt searched online for a product similar to what she had envisioned. When she did not find anything, she sewed her own prototypes and tested them at home. Luckily, she had started a production company years before her injury. Weisblatt used her connections and had a small quantity manufactured. She marketed using promos and giveaways on parent and baby blogs. "The main concern was my Pacifier Snappy and that it was too long," she said. Based on her consumer responses, Weisblatt began researching the Consumer Product Safety Commission's standard of length for baby products. Weisblatt reduced the length of the Snappy so it met those standards and reflected her consumer feedback. She also added extra snaps to the Snappy so it could be shortened when not being used.

Now Weisblatt runs a successful baby product company called Bubele, which means "sweet baby." Her brainchild has grown from selling Pacifier Snappys to selling baby clothes and products of all kinds.

INTELLECTUAL PROPERTY PROTECTION

Weisblatt filed a provisional patent application so she could test the market for one year and be protected. "When the provisional was about to expire, I applied for the full patent and, after a lot of going back and forth with required info with the USPTO, they are still under review." Weisblatt's advice to beginning inventors: "Lay out a very detailed plan before you start so that you can research every single detail. This will allow you to predict problems before they occur. Unfortunately, I learned many lessons the hard way as I went along."

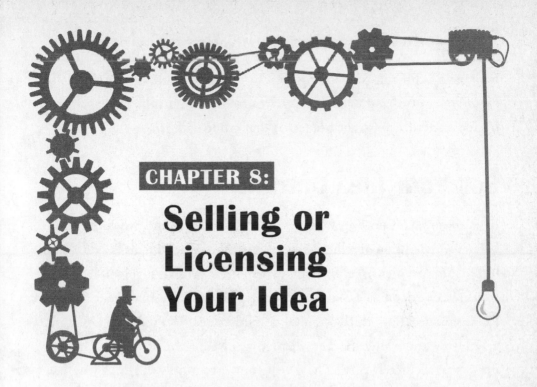

CHAPTER 8:

Selling or Licensing Your Idea

"The march of invention has clothed mankind with powers of which a century ago the boldest imagination could not have dreamt."

— HENRY GEORGE, AUTHOR

You have a few options when it comes to commercializing your invention. The first is to sell your idea outright to another entity, which will then own rights to your idea and invention. The second option is to license your idea to another entity. Your third option is to maintain control and produce the invention yourself. *See Chapters 9 and 10 for more information.*

There are pros and cons to each of these routes, and it is not a decision to take lightly. You first need to decide how much control you want to have over the commercialization process. If this invention is your life's work, you may have a difficult time letting go. On the other hand, if you decide to maintain control and commercialize yourself, you must be ready to run a business and deal with the headaches that come with it.

Sell Your Idea Outright

If you know you do not want to run a business around your invention, you have the option of selling the idea outright, which involves a one-time lump-sum payment, or licensing your idea, which involves receiving royalties based on sales. Invention and product licensing agent Harvey Reese says deciding which option is best for you is "…a judgment call, and you'll only know after the fact whether you were right or wrong." There is no way to accurately predict how well your invention will sell. If you have done your research and fulfilled a need in the public sphere, your product is more likely to be successful. However, other factors are unpredictable in terms of the how successful the product will be.

This a daunting statistic, but one to keep in mind as you decide what route you take in commercialization. If you decide to take a licensing deal (i.e., get paid royalties based on sales) and the product is one of the 85 percent that do not succeed in the marketplace, then you will not make much on royalties. On the other hand, if you have an invention that turns out to be a huge success and you sell the idea outright (i.e., lump sum up front), you might make far less than you would from royalties. For example, Hasbro bought the rights to the G.I. Joe doll for $100,000. Because of the specific terms and agreements in the contract, the inventor makes no royalties from this product and has lost out on millions. There was no way for the inventor to know that the doll would be so successful — and would still be selling 40 years after entering the marketplace.

Keep this in mind when you decide whether to sell your idea outright or license your idea. As Reese advises, "All you can do is weigh the facts available at the time, trust your instincts, and pray that you make the right decision."

License Your Idea

If you do not want to maintain control of the process of commercialization or if you just prefer idea development, then licensing your idea may be the best route for you. Obtaining a licensing agreement is quite difficult. According to Dr. Pamela Riddle Bird, founder of the Inventors Educational Foundation, only about 6 percent of inventors succeed in getting their products licensed. Another study shows slightly higher numbers: Ron Westrum, a professor of sociology at Eastern Michigan University, and Ed Zimmer showed that 13 percent of one-patent inventors successfully sold a license for their products. However, some experts believe this number is high as a result of the type of people who responded to the study — those who were unsuccessful were less likely to respond to the mailed survey, according to Nolo.com.

Licensing your idea means you enter into a contractual agreement granting rights to your intellectual property. You will give the licensee the right to make a product based on your patent, but you will keep the rights to that product. The licensee could be a manufacturer, a marketer, an individual, or anyone willing to pay you to let them take the product to market. You will get royalties from the product's sales,and whatever other compensation you include in your licensing agreement. An example of licensing is the board game Monopoly, created during the Great Depression by Charles Darrow. He designed the game and licensed the rights to Parker Brothers.

Darrow did not ever have to work again, and his heirs are still collecting on his royalty payments. In this case, licensing likely made Mr. Darrow (and the generations to follow) more money than they would have made by selling the idea outright.

To License or Not to License

There are many factors you will need to look at in order to decide what is best for you and your product. An advantage to licensing your product is you will have less responsibility in the day-to-day business, and your product will probably get to market much quicker. The cost of manufacturing and developing the product may be significant, and having a licensing partner who can send your invention straight to quality production may improve its chances of success. The sooner it hits the shelves, the sooner you will start earning royalties.

The disadvantage to licensing your product is you will have a lower earning potential than manufacturing it on your own — you are likely not going to make millions from a licensing agreement. It may take much longer to manufacture your product if you do it yourself, but you will earn more when it does hit shelves.

Here are some more things to think about when making your decision:

> **Do you have business experience?** If yes, your experience may help you understand the difficulty of keeping control of your product. However, having no business experience does not disqualify you from manufacturing your own invention. Just keep in mind that becoming an entrepreneur is going to come with frustrations, especially if you do not have much experience.

> **Do you already have ideas for other inventions stewing?** If you are a creative mind and are eager to start working on your next project, think about licensing.

> **Are you a good manager?** As an entrepreneur, you are going to have to manage a number of things at once, including manufacturing, marketing, sales, customer service and more — or manage the people who manage those areas once you get larger. This takes a great deal of commitment, organization, and time-management skills.

Advantages of Licensing

> Licensing gives you more resources to develop your invention. The licensee, especially if it is a big firm, has the resources to put teams of professionals to work on getting your invention on the market. What would be a huge undertaking for one person will not seem as large to them.

> The licensee can help you see things about your product you might not have noticed. The licensee probably has more business experience than you do and will bring another point of insight to your project.

> You might get some money upfront from the license.

Disadvantages of Licensing

> You have to give up most, if not all, of your control over your product, its development, and its marketing. If you are still giving input, it is usually just as a consultant.

> Finding a licensee is not easy, and finding a good one can be even tougher.

> ➤ You obviously want to protect your interests, but this can be difficult once you decide to go the way of licensing. Negotiating with licensees can be complicated, and they usually will have greater resources than you. You might have to look into hiring a lawyer to represent you.

Getting the Licensing Deal

You've decided. You want to license your product and have someone else manufacture it. You are ready to proceed to the following steps. Remember that getting the licensing deal is not going to be easy. You must find a licensee and prove why your product is worth spending the money on.

Finding a licensee

First, you need to find an individual or company to which to license your product. Also, find a business your product will benefit. If possible, find a manufacturing business rather than just a retailer. It will be easier for you to make the sale to the manufacturing business — they are more likely to see the product's potential. For example, if you have created a new type of safety mirror for a vehicle, it would be easier to sell that mirror to a car manufacturer rather than a retailer because the car manufacturer would benefit from adding the newest safety feature to its vehicles.

When shopping for a company to license and mass-produce your product, remember to look for a candidate that can develop and make your product but that can also sell your product the best. The success of your invention is really about finding the best-suited all-around partner. In order to make money, your product has to sell. One company might be the best developer of your product, but if it cannot sell it, you are not going to make any money. How much you earn from royalties is dependent on the sales the product generates.

Some places to start:

➢ Look back at the list of competitors you created in the Action Step in Chapter 2. Check to see who makes those products and who distributes them. Visit the websites of the manufacturers and distributors to learn about the companies, and contact them if they seem like a good fit.

➢ Read the Thomas Register®, a set of books with contact information for U.S. manufacturers. These books are available in the reference section at the library, or you can obtain the Thomas Register on CD by calling 800-222-7900 or visiting the website (**www.thomasnct. com**).

➢ Attend trade shows to meet potential licensees. Trade shows are designed to exhibit new advancements in the industry. They are industry-specific and will get you face-to-face with potential licensees. They are also a good place to examine the industry — the new technology, new products, and new inventors.

Contacting potential licensees

Obtaining the names of the potential licensees was the easy part. The more difficult task is getting a meeting with them. You have to convince the company you are worth listening to. At this point, you want to begin to call these potential licensees. Reese advises that when you call, ask to speak with the president of the company — and if that is not possible, then the second in command.

When you get the contact on the phone, explain who you are and what you want, politely and briefly. You do not want to give away too much information in this phone call because you want to ensure you get an appointment to make your pitch.

If you cannot get in touch with the right people, the other option is to put together a letter to send out to potential licensees. In the letter, provide a description of your invention and how it the potential licensee will benefit from the product. Do not disclose exact information or specifications about your invention, however.

Developing your pitch

You need to develop a presentation on your invention. If you decide that licensing is the route you wish to go, your goal is to show the potential licensee the value in your idea. Your presentation needs to include a few key points:

> An overview of your invention — what it does and how it does it. Discuss *how* it is better than anything on the market (not just *that* it is better). Explain the processes (if there are any) in simple, easy-to-understand terms.

> Discuss any intellectual property protection that you have, are working on, or plan to obtain.

> Present an analysis of the market. Be sure to show there is a market for your product.

> Give details about production, costs, sales projections, profit margins, marketing and any other related information.

Be careful not to "oversell" your idea by being overly ambitious. Do not use phrases such as "This is the product the world has been waiting for," or "My invention will change the world." Simply explain your invention and show the value in it. Keep in mind that the potential licensee has the goal of making a profit off of your product, so focus your presentation on showing how your invention can do this. Also, if your product complements another product the potential licensee makes, make a note.

Assess the licensee

Once you have found a potential candidate to license your product to, do your research on that candidate. Make sure the potential licensee is suitable for marketing your product. Do a background check of violations, lawsuits, and complaints. You are entering into a partnership with this candidate, so you want to make sure you know everything you need to know about them before you put your product and your product's future in the licensee's hands.

Richard Levy, who has licensed more than 125 inventions including the Furby, says he has had companies not honor their licensing contracts on inventions with all levels of success. You must feel secure with the company with which you enter an agreement. "No amount of money or level of royalty/guarantee is worth taking unless you feel 100 percent confident in the company, its honesty, stability, and ability to deliver on the specific performance required by the contract. Contracts are only as good as the people who sign them," Levy says.

Negotiating a deal

Take time before meeting with potential licensees to decide things such as whether the license will be exclusive or nonexclusive. **Exclusive licensing** means the licensing is only given to one company while **nonexclusive licensing** allows licensing rights to multiple companies at once. If exclusive, how long will it be exclusive? Decide what quality and performance guarantees you expect from the licensee. Do a strengths, weaknesses, opportunities, and threats (SWOT) analysis. A **SWOT analysis** is a technique used by licensing experts in which they analyze and evaluate the intellectual properties of the product. Each of the four areas will be analyzed in relation to your product. The strengths and weaknesses analyze your product while the opportunities and threats consider the market surrounding your product. When negotiating a deal with the licensee, be prepared to answer questions regarding the strengths, weaknesses, opportunities, and threats of your product. These are areas the potential licensee will want to cover when trying to determine whether your product would be profitable.

Now you are ready to sign the deal and get your product closer to production. Again, make sure you have the rights to your patent protected in any agreement you sign with anyone regarding the product. The licensing agreement should not only protect your patent rights and assure your royalties, but it also should cover the trademarks and copyrights regarding the product. The licensing company still makes a large amount of money off of the invention, paying you royalties, or a portion of every sale. It is advisable to have an attorney draw up or at least look over the agreement before you sign it.

The following information should be included in your license agreement.

PAYMENT INFORMATION

This includes information about royalties paid by the licensee to you, the inventor. According to Reese, this is usually 5 to 10 percent. This number is negotiable, but do not sell yourself short or get greedy. There should also be information about the frequency with which payments will be made. Most licensing agreements also include information about an advance payment, also negotiable. Specifically, the agreement should include the following information:

> **Royalty rate:** A royalty is the share of the profit you as the inventor will receive from the company to which you assign the license. The royalty rate varies among different industries. For example, in the toy industry, royalties generally range from 4 to 15 percent, according to Furby inventor Levy. To calculate your royalty, you need to know the net price per unit and the royalty rate. The licensee may also give you projected sales for the upcoming year so you can calculate the projected royalty for that year. For example, if the net price of one unit is $20 and your royalty is 8 percent, you will make $1.60 off each unit sold. Be sure the agreement states precisely how the royalty will be calculated as opposed to just saying a percentage of net sales.

When Don Kracke, author of *Turn Your Idea or Invention into Millions*, sold the license to Rubbermaid® for the Con-Tact brand shelf liners, he agreed to a royalty rate of 2.5 percent because of the narrow profit margin for the product. Between May of 1986 and November of 2000, Kracke received a grand total of $1,303,620.98. So keep in mind the volume of sales and the price point when determining the royalty rate.

> **Advances:** These are upfront payments and are not part of all licensing agreements. If you can get an advance, it will put money in your pocket immediately. Advances are given at the contract signing or in payments throughout the first year. The larger the advance, the better. Levy advises that the advance should be one-third to one-fourth of the projected royalties for the first year (based on sales). Using the example above (royalty rate of 8 percent and net price of one unit is $20, giving you $1.60 for each unit sold), factor in that the company predicts 100,000 units sold in the first year. Therefore your advance should be one-third or one-fourth of that figure (i.e., you would make $160,000 in royalties for the first year). So your advance would be between $40,000 (one-fourth) or $52,800 (one-third).

Licensing agent Reese notes that in his experience with licensing, which includes more than 100 of his own ideas, in 25 percent of the licensing agreements, no actual product is ever manufactured. If this happens, you (the inventor) will likely end up with the rights to the idea, which you can try to sell again to another company. Having an advance at least guarantees some compensation.

Levy also cautions that a lower advance or no advance at all can be an indication of the backing you have from the company. "For example, if you are paid $1,000, it is much easier for a licensee to deep-six your project, say in the face of a manufacturing problem, than if it had paid $100,000. The greater the financial commitment, the more reason the company has to make the product go," he says. In other words, the lower an advance is, the less investment a company has in an invention, and the quicker it may cancel it.

> **Deductions:** Whether the upfront payment amount will be deducted from royalties (i.e., is it a "bonus" or is it an pre-payment of future royalties?).

> **Calculation:** The method for calculating royalties, which should be gross or net sales.

> **Guarantees:** Sometimes you can negotiate a guaranteed minimum for royalties. This will give you a minimum amount of money you will make from royalties in a specific time.

> **Schedule for payments:** How often you will be paid (e.g., monthly).

> **Methods:** How you, the inventor, will check the sales information (i.e., auditing and verifying).

> **Insurance:** What the inventor can do if not paid on time.

> **Fees:** For consulting, etc (i.e., keeping you — the inventor — on board to answer questions and assist).

RIGHTS INFORMATION

This includes information about who will maintain rights to various aspects of the invention. The rights usually addressed are patent(s), copyrights, trademarks, and trade secrets.

> **Transferability of the agreement**: If the company sells the line to another company, you still want to get paid.

➤ **Time period for the license:** Some companies may try to put a limit on the time you will receive royalties for your invention. For example, when the patent expires, you would stop receiving royalties. However, as you can see from the Monopoly example above, some inventions will continue to sell well for years past the patent expiration. If you set a time on the royalties, you could lose a lot of money. If the company pushes for a set time period, Levy suggests you opt for a clause in the contract says if there is a solid decline in the sales of your invention, your royalty rate will go down. For example, assume your original royalty rate was 8 percent, but your patent has expired and a competitor has entered the market, causing sales to go down. At this point, your original rate would decrease.

➤ **Back-out clause:** The company might want a clause in the agreement saying it can back out. For example, if the company is not making money or even losing money on the invention, it might want to pull out of the deal and just pay the royalties that are due. The rights will transfer back to the inventor. This can be two-sided, with a clause such as "Either party may terminate the agreement with 30 days' written notice…"

➤ **Territory limitations:** This is the scope of the license in terms of geographic boundaries. Harvey Reese says he limits the scope of his license agreements to the United States, Canada, and Mexico. He advises that if the company is an international company, expand the territory. If not, stick with the United States, Canada, and Mexico.

RESPONSIBILITIES

> **Pursuing infringers:** Intellectual property protection does not guarantee someone will not try to copy your idea. You must be on the lookout for infringers and pursue legal action against those infringers. If you enter into a licensing agreement, include a clause about whether you as the inventor or the licensee will go after intellectual property infringers.

> **Liability:** If there should happen to be any lawsuits against your product, be sure you will not be held responsible. For example, a small piece on the Burpee Baby Bottle comes loose and an infant chokes on it and dies. The parents file a lawsuit. Does the lawsuit fall on you as the inventor or on the licensee as the manufacturer? It depends on the licensing agreement. If the liability falls on you in the agreement, be sure to have insurance protecting you.

> **Patent protection:** In this part of the licensing contract, you will need to determine who will pay for the patent if it has not been obtained yet and whose name the patent will be in.

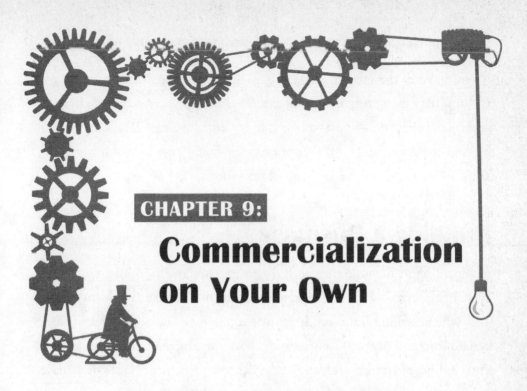

CHAPTER 9

Commercialization on Your Own

"Want is the mistress of invention."

— SUSANNA CENTLIVRE, BRITISH POET

If you decide to manufacture the invention yourself, know that the cost of creating an invention can be substantial and overwhelming. Your costs thus far might have included design assistance, a patent agent or attorney, the patent application, and prototype production — not to mention the time commitment you have invested in your invention. The costs will continue to add up during the next stages. You will need funds to actually produce the products you will sell. You will also need money for marketing and advertising, business cards, a website, and patent maintenance fees. Where do you get this money?

If you have all the money yourself, you are already on your way, and you will not have many financial obstacles. However, if you need some help — and most people do — you will need to try other avenues. This chapter will explain the two main funding options: self-financing your own invention and finding outside funding from other sources.

Building a Business

By deciding to manufacture and distribute your invention on your own, you are also making the decision to run a business around your invention. You will be selling your product; maintaining financial records; finding distributors and distribution channels; handling the marketing, advertising and public relations; and the list goes on. You can hire salespeople, accountants, distributors, and marketing employees — but at a cost. You might not have envisioned this side of the invention process as being for you, but if you cannot find a licensee or an entity to buy your idea, this might be the only route you are left with.

Entire books are written about starting businesses, and though this is not the focus of this book, an overview is necessary. You need to know what to look forward to as a business owner, some of which you may never have thought of. Maintaining control of your business is not all glamour. Being your own boss does give you freedom, but it also means you have to be extremely diligent. Your entire life will likely begin to revolve around your business, and you may end up working more hours in a day than you are used to, especially in the beginning.

According to Harvey Reese, there are five important components to a successful business (in order of importance): sufficient capital or funds;

understanding of business operations; unending energy and heart; devotion to the industry; and finally, a good idea.

Pamela Riddle Bird, Ph.D., founder and CEO of Innovative Product Technologies, Inc., says to start a business, "you need a whole range of skills that very few people have." A business owner must be a "financial wiz, a marketing genius, a winning salesperson, an efficient production manager, an empathetic human resources manager, and a reliable truck driver," in addition to having creativity, determination, and persistence. You must also consider the huge risk you are taking when starting a business. The Small Business Administration says 50 percent of small businesses fail in the first five years. Your product may be up against competitors with seemingly unending resources.

When you license your idea, you need not worry about things like manufacturing and distribution. Licensing provides the opportunity to have someone else plan for those things. But when you maintain control of your idea, you are responsible for the manufacturing, distribution, marketing, customer service, and so on.

Financing

Any business, of course, needs capital. Here are the two ways you can go about finding the money to make your invention become a reality.

Self-financing

If you have the funds to try it on your own, take the path of self-financing. It gives you the most control over your invention. If you go this route, you are using your own savings, credit cards, personal credit loans, home equity loans, or retirement funds. This path is riddled with risk because you potentially could lose everything — your savings, your home, or anything else you use to generate funds.

Obtain outside funding

If using your own money (or personal credit) is too much to stomach, you have other options for getting money to produce your invention yourself without giving up total control over it. Bank loans must be paid back, of course, according to the terms on which they are lent. On the other hand, you also may be able to borrow or solicit investments from your family and friends. Keep in mind when seeking investments from family and friends that these investments give them partial ownership of your enterprise. The best role for family-and-friend funding is in product development. This is the most speculative phase of your business, one unlikely to qualify for investment funding or loans from other sources.

If you have good credit — or even decent credit — you might want to look for a small-business loan. It is difficult for a start-up business to obtain a regular loan from a bank because of the likelihood that new business will fail, but the U.S. Small Business Administration (SBA) has loan programs for small-business people to help them obtain bank financing (**www.sba.gov/services/financialassistance**). The SBA facilitates many different types of loans. These loans are not from the SBA itself but are made and financed through commercial lending institutions, with the SBA guaranteeing them.

7(A) LOAN PROGRAM

According to the SBA, these loans are the most flexible and can be used by start-up and existing small businesses for general business functions. The major types of 7(a) loans are:

➤ **Express Programs:** Express loans are for specific borrowers. The loan process is simplified and accelerated.

➤ **Export Loan Programs:** These are special loans for small businesses that export products.

➤ **Rural Lender Advantage Program:** This SBA initiative targets banks in small or rural communities by streamlining the process so it is easier for them to make business loans.

➤ **Special Purpose Loans Program:** These are for small businesses that need loans to assist with specific circumstances, such as job losses tied to the North American Free Trade Agreement (NAFTA), seasonal or short-term capital needs, pollution controls, and Employee Stock Ownership Plans.

CDC/504 LOAN PROGRAM

A Certified Development Company (CDC) is a nonprofit organization that assists with economic development in its community. According to the SBA, the CDC/504 Loan Program "provides long-term, fixed-rate financing to acquire fixed assets (such as real estate or equipment) for expansion or modernization."

MICROLOAN PROGRAM

The SBA's Microloan Program offers loans up to $35,000. These loans are short term with the purpose of providing small businesses with money for supplies, machinery, equipment, inventory, or furniture.

Partberships

If you have a few friends, business associates, or family members who believe in you and might want to invest in your invention, you might want to think about a partnership. A partnership is more than just asking someone you know if you can borrow money. Instead, a partnership allows the person to be part of the processes and decisions for the invention.

If you have created an invention with someone else, you have a co-inventor. Co-inventorship is a precarious status because either inventor can license or assign the rights to the invention and profit solely from it without the partner's consent or even knowledge. An agreement signed upfront designating the rights of each co-inventor will prevent misunderstandings and hard feelings down the road.

Some inventors turn to business partners with the aim of drumming up more investment in their new start-up and becoming more business-savvy. These partners should bring contacts, experience, and expertise in areas critical to the growing startup. They also should be people you are willing to work closely with. As with straight investments, or stock and partnership investments, check the implications from securities laws before you take on business partners.

Have a formal arrangement with your potential investors, no matter who they are. This will protect everyone involved and allow for resolution up front if any problems arise. The three main aspects of the agreement should be time, control, and money. Time clarifies how much time each partner commits to the business. Control defines what each partner is responsible for, such as the operation of the company and minor business decisions. Money concerns investments by each partner and the distribution of profits/losses.

There are two main types of partnerships: general partnership and limited partnership. It is always best to have a written partnership agreement, even though it is not legally necessary. If you use an attorney to draft the agreement, it can range from between $500 to $2,000.

> **A general partnership** is a business arrangement where two or more people run a business together as co-owners, sharing responsibilities as well as financial obligation (profits and losses).

> A **limited partnership** has two different types of partners. It includes at least one managing partner who runs the business. The other type of partner is a limited partner who contributes funds but is not involved in the operation of the business.

Government programs

Another route to find funding might be through government programs such as grants and loans. Several government branches award grants and loans as a way to help fund research and even develop inventions. However, obtaining a government grant is a long, difficult process. It will take plenty of research and hard work because these grants tend to be quite specific about the type of qualifying invention. You also want to pay attention to government stipulations on royalties and other rights regarding development of the invention.

The Small Business Association is a great source of information about government loans and grants. You can visit the SBA website at **www.sba.gov**. The SBA can help you get qualified for a loan when you are not able to get funding on your own. The SBA has two grant programs: the Small Business Innovation Research Program (SBIR) and the Small Business Technology Transfer Program (STTR).

Eleven government branches participate in the SBIR, including the U.S. Department of Education, which says the program "funds research and development projects that propose a sound approach to the investigation of an important education or assistive technology, science, or engineering question under topics identified each year in the solicitation." To qualify for a SBIR program, you must be a for-profit, independent American company with no more than 500 employees. SBIR has state affiliates that can help inventors locally. Find out more about the program at **www.sbir.gov**.

As for STTR, according to the SBA website, "STTR's most important role is to foster the innovation necessary to meet the nation's scientific and technological challenges in the 21st century." The SBIR does not require a partnership with a university or nonprofit research organization, but the STTR does. Just like with the SBIR, small businesses that participate in the STTR must be for-profit, independent American companies with fewer than 500 employees. According to the SBA website, "Each year, five federal departments and agencies are required by STTR to reserve a portion of their research and development funds for award to small business/nonprofit research institution partnerships: Department of Defense, Department of Energy, Department of Health and Human Services, National Aeronautics and Space Administration, and National Science Foundation."

The SBA is not your only stop for government grants, though. The U.S. Department of Energy's inventions program sometimes provides funding and technical assistance to alternative energy inventors, and the U.S. Department of Agriculture provides grants to inventors of agricultural products.

FOUNDATION GRANTS

Other sources of grant money can be foundations created by larger organizations and companies. For example, Motorola sponsors the

Innovation Generation Grants, which award more than $5 million for young inventors in Pre-K through 12th grade. In addition, the National Collegiate Inventors and Innovators Alliance (NCIIA) awards grants from $1,000 to $50,000 to faculty and students of colleges and universities. According to the NCIIA website, grants are awarded to "support innovation, invention, and entrepreneurship" (**http://nciia.org/grants**). These companies are seeking new products for production and distribution. Your local library might even have some directories for companies such as these. However, you will need to have a few facts about your product or invention before you approach these foundations. For instance, you will need to know an estimate of how much it will cost to produce your invention, as well as a ballpark estimate of profit generated for the company. A company interested in giving a grant will want to know information like this before considering investing in your product. Local inventors or entrepreneurial organizations might be a good source of information about local grant money. For information about area grants, another great resource is your local college or university.

VENTURE CAPITAL

Venture capital is a type of vested funding. It typically comes from numerous individuals or entities who pool their money and invest in a company or product that shows promise in generating a significant return or profit. Venture capitalists are investors who provide capital to help new businesses get off the ground. They can invest anywhere from $100,000 to $50 million or more, depending on how much the start-up needs and how much potential they see. They will often help bring an invention to the market; however, this can be quite costly to you as the inventor or patent holder. Often, in return for lending you money, the investors will require stock or an ownership percentage in the company or product. On the other hand, the investors are usually seasoned business people who have many resources at their disposal. The investors will have much at stake financially with your company or product, so they may be willing to help you find customers for the product and even employees or business partners, if needed.

Many books can help you find venture capitalists. These can be found in the reference section of a library. Examples include Pratt's *Guide to Venture Capital Sources, The Directory of Venture Capital and Private Equity Firms,* and *Fitzroy Dearborn International Directory of Venture Capital Funds.* Also, check out the vFinance® website (**www.vfinance.com**).

If you decide to go with venture capital as the funding source to mass-produce your product, you likely will have to go before several venture capital groups and make presentations to show the value and potential of your product. The reason for giving multiple presentations is because the funding comes from various sources. Your proposed business or product will have to be approved by several different groups within the investment pool; some venture capitalists are individuals, and some are made up of multiple people/firms.

Do plenty of research before you even schedule your first presentation. For example, you will need to be able to give a realistic estimate of future earnings. It is a good idea to give profit-earning estimates for six-month periods over about two years. This will help venture capitalists have a better idea of the potential for your product over the next two years.

In order to determine the profit you will make, you will need to know the overall cost to manufacture the product. Have a guideline for not only the production, but also the development and distribution of the product. If you do not know how to determine this on your own, hire an expert or consult trusted business friends as to how to go about doing this. You will need to decide whether you will manufacture the entire product or instead outsource part of it and then assemble it; what type of equipment you will need to produce the product; and how many products you will be able to produce at a time. You will need to do extensive research, know what your options are, and know which options will best suit your product.

You also need to have a business plan to present to the venture capitalists. In this business plan, show that the product has a market and that there is a demand for the product. You need to know the cost of production and how much you will be able to charge for the product. Determine how much people will be willing to pay for your product by finding similar products and seeing how much they sell for. Know what kind of profit you will have when you deduct the cost of production from the actual retail price.

It is also wise to recognize the obstacles and difficulties you might face when producing or distributing the product. Know ahead of time how you would handle these situations. Give examples of how you would overcome various obstacles that may occur. Above all, you will need a prototype of the product to show the investors. Prove to the investors that you have done your research and understand the business associated with your product. These types of investors are notorious for investing only in products and businesses that show a high degree of growth potential. Venture companies want to see significant returns on the money they lend, usually about 20 percent per year. They need to see commitment to making the production of your invention a complete success.

If they accept, you will enter into an agreement or contract with the venture capitalists. Included in the contract might be the venture capitalists' right to take over your company under certain circumstances, such as rapidly falling sales or other problems. If there is uncertainty about your invention's success or your ability to run the company, even slightly, the venture capitalists might want to include this in the contract. Sometimes, the venture capitalists will have a large stake — even more than half — of the company. In addition, the contract may include a clause that the venture capitalists can pull out if specified milestones are not met. The stronger your product and the information you present, the better leverage you will have in negotiating a contract.

Deciding to manufacture your own product using funds from venture capitalists does require you to give up some control of the product and business. Although most venture capitalists remain in the background for most of the day-to-day decisions, they might insist on making changes if things do not go as anticipated. In addition, venture capitalists often want to invest in publicly-traded companies. If you want to keep your company a family-run business, venture capitalists might not be the best route. Obtaining small-business loans and keeping the business under your control would be best.

CASE STUDY: THE HOTDOG EZ BUN STEAMER® AND THE STEAMIE

Chris Schutte
http://hotdogezbunsteamer.com
http://steaminggrills.com

For as long as he could remember, Chris Schutte always wanted to be an inventor. Raised by a single mom who saved money on food by freezing everything, he watched her bring frozen buns back to life in her 1960s-style dome steamer. Years later, while trying to duplicate the stadium-style hot dogs available at sporting events, he realized the secret to a great hot dog was steamed buns. That is when he remembered his mom's bun steamer and thought, "If she could bring back to life six-month-old frozen buns, there has to be an easy way to make a fresh-tasting ballpark hot dog at home. I'm already boiling the hot dog in water. Why can't I steam the buns at the same time?" That is how The Hotdog EZ Bun Steamer concept was born.

NAPKIN SKETCH TO WORKING PROTOTYPE

Schutte started by placing a cheese grater on top of the pot that hot dogs were boiling in. It did not quite work, and he realized that the buns needed to be down in the pot so a lid could cover them. He sketched an idea for a grill that hung from the rim of the pot with adjustable hooked handles and headed off to the local hardware store to buy the $30 in parts needed to build a prototype. His initial design produced a fantastic hot dog bun, but the grill blocked access to the hot dog meat below, making it awkward to use. He realized if he added a cross-shaped opening in the grill, the hot dogs would drop through into the water and the buns would sit above the boiling water. When the dogs are cooked, they can be retrieved with a pair of tongs through the opening in the grill. At that moment in August 2003, Schutte knew he had a million dollar idea. He built and tested a second prototype with the cross-shaped opening and discovered it worked perfectly.

CREATING A BUSINESS PLAN

Schutte spent the next few years working 60+ hours a week at his full-time job in sales and marketing for a national consumer electronic retailer. He found himself spending every spare minute reading about the inventing and patenting process. When the economy started to decline, the company he worked for struggled to stay in business. In July 2007, Schutte was laid off from his corporate job and now had all the time he needed to develop his product. While getting started, he knew he needed a business plan and IP (intellectual property) protection. He turned to friends and family for advice and financial support. That is how he found out about Google Patent Search and SCORE, a group of retired business executives that volunteer their time to advise entrepreneurs and business owners. Schutte's initial plan called for raising $30,000 by selling 30-percent interest in the concept to friends and family. He used that money to secure the patents and trademarks needed to protect the idea before trying to bring it to market.

That summer he spent most of his time writing his business plan and researching patent attorneys. After all his patent searches came back with no conflicting pre-existing patents, he started collecting the money from investors and formed the partnership, Innovative Everyday Products, LLC.

MANUFACTURING

Like most inventors, Schutte hoped to license his idea to an existing housewares manufacturer and collect royalties. However, all of the experts he consulted with said if you really want to see your invention in the marketplace, you have to be prepared to manufacture, market, and distribute your invention yourself. Schutte started soliciting every housewares manufacturer he could find, but most never responded. It was quickly looking like the experts were right.

Using the website ThomasNet (**www.ThomasNet.com**), Schutte found an American company that manufactured similar products and contacted them about manufacturing a sample production run. Schutte knew his first big opportunity to market his invention would be at the 2008 International Home and Housewares Show in Chicago, which at that point was only a few months away.

At this point, an inventor learns about the 1 to 5 manufacturing cost to retail ratio. If it costs $1.00 to make, the customers need to be willing to purchase it for $5.00. Schutte thought the most a consumer would pay for his Hotdog Steamer was $19.95, but Schutte's manufacturer came back with a production cost of $19 each. Using the 1 to 5 rule, he knew customers were not going to pay $95 for his hotdog bun steamer, so he decided to contact the production manager directly to find out what could be done. The production manager told him the way the handles attached to the grill was difficult to produce, and a minor design change could cut the manufacturing cost in half. With the new handle attachment design approved, the first manufactured prototype was produced for testing.

A month later and with only three months remaining before the show, the first manufactured prototype showed up. After some testing, it quickly became clear the handles did not perform well holding the lid in place on a wide range of pot styles and Chris found himself facing his second hurdle. The only way to have functioning inventory on hand in time for the housewares show was to fly to Houston and drive two hours to personally meet with the production manager at the factory in Shiner, Texas. He pulled up to the door of this 140-year-old factory, and once the production manager understood what the problem was, a solution was only a few hours away.

MARKET RESEARCH AND PRODUCT DEVELOPMENT

Chris believed he had a marketable idea, but he still needed some unbiased market research to prove he had a viable product. With a limited budget, Schutte decided to make hot dogs for the on-duty firemen at several local fire stations. While he cooked using The Hotdog EZ Bun Steamer, his wife asked them market research questions and recorded their answers.

With a few hundred manufactured units to sell and market research in hand, Schutte and his wife headed off to the 2008 International Home and Housewares Show in Chicago. Their booth was in an area called The Inventors Corner and was fertile ground for the news reporters covering the show. That night, Schutte and his wife watched the TV as their product was one of only four products featured on the evening news. For a new inventor trying to promote his product, getting on the news was a pretty good start.

Now that Schutte was actually selling the Hotdog EZ Bun Steamer, he started receiving customer feedback. His customers wanted a larger design and wanted to know what else the device could steam. He immediately developed a larger version of the Hotdog EZ Bun Steamer, and as soon as it was available, his customers started talking about all the other foods they were steaming with it.

Building on the publicity from appearing on the Chicago evening news, Schutte was able to land a deal with QVC, an online shopping company. In August 2009, he became a certified QVC guest host and presented his invention on national TV. The thrill of appearing on live TV was quickly squashed when the sales results turned out to be far below his minimum expectations. Reviewing the video from the TV appearance and carefully listening to the customer's feedback, Schutte started making design changes to take his product to the next level.

The first thing he did was make the opening in the grill keyhole-shaped so it could hold a small sauce dish. Because so many customers reported they were using the grill to steam tortillas, he added a center piece so tortillas larger than the diameter of the pot could be steamed. He also noticed that lifting the grill out of the pot with oven mitts was awkward, so he added heat-resistant silicone finger pads to the handles, which made it easy to handle the hot grill. Next, he added a clip-on steaming basket so smaller vegetables could be steamed, and as a bonus feature, it could also deep-fry. The last thing he did was change the name to "The Steamie," which was simple and said it all.

When Schutte combined the grill, the sauce dish, and the clip-on steaming basket into a single three-piece kit, it was an instant hit with everyone he showed it to. Returning to the 2010 International Home and Housewares Show, The Steamie three-piece system was extremely well received. Now there were two distinct products and two market strategies. The Hotdog EZ Bun Steamer® was best suited to become a clip strip product hanging next to the hotdog buns in every grocery store in America, while The Steamie with its many multiple uses was better suited to be sold and demonstrated on TV.

MARKETING

Building on the publicity from appearing on the Chicago evening news and QVC, Schutte contacted the public relations department for LegalZoom.com and pitched the idea to appear in their next round of TV commercials. The marketing department liked how Chris used several different LegalZoom.com online services to develop his Hotdog EZ Bun Steamer® concept and decided to include him in a new TV commercial. The result was one of LegalZoom.com's most effective TV commercials and millions of dollars of free advertising for Schutte and his product.

Looking to garner more media attention, in June 2010, Schutte attended the Inpex Invention Show in Pittsburgh where he pitched The Steamie in front of a panel of direct response TV experts. By a unanimous decision, the expert panel sent Schutte and The Steamie to the New Product Showcase at the 2010 Annual Electronic Retailers Association's Conference & Exposition trade show. At the show, there were 40 pre-selected inventors pitching their products to a panel of judges and infomercial experts. The Steamie was judged the best new product of the show, and Schutte was named The 2010 ERA Moxie Award Winner for Inventor of the Year.

The notoriety generated from being named Inventor of the Year led to articles in newspapers from San Francisco to Atlanta. When LegalZoom.com found out their TV pitchman was selected Inventor of the Year, they asked Schutte to record a national radio commercial to capitalize on his success.

DISTRIBUTION

Distribution is difficult, but its the most important aspect of the product development process an inventor needs to conquer. Free TV commercials, newspaper articles, and national awards mean nothing if they do not translate into sales, and the only way to get sales is through distribution. Before an inventor starts building distribution, he or she needs to have a winning go-to market strategy. Inventors need to understand where their product fits in the marketplace and how to best present it.

Nowadays, the best place for an inventor to start selling a product is on eBay, Amazon.com, or similar websites. Setup is easy, and you can quickly learn at which price point your product sells best and how it needs to be shipped. The next step would be to set up your own website. After Schutte developed his own website, the next place he took his product was to mail order catalog companies. Because these companies sell products online or through catalogs, retail packaging is not necessary. A plain box and a good product picture is all you need. In the case of The Steamie, however, the multi-function steaming capabilities were lost in a single picture and really needed a video demonstration to be successful.

From the beginning, Schutte believed The Hotdog EZ Bun Steamer would be most successful hanging next to the buns in the bread aisle of every grocery store in America. He was able to identify two main players in the grocery store clip strip business. After a quick pitch, a deal was struck to test market the Hotdog EZ Bun Steamer in a few hundred grocery stores at the end of 2010.

As for The Steamie, QVC asked Chris to create a four-piece version, including the Hotdog EZ Bun Steamer, and present it on QVC in February 2011. Finally, after three years of trials and tribulation, Schutte was able to negotiate a licensing deal with a media company that produces infomercials. In the spring of 2011, The Steamie Genie is test marketing to see if it has what it takes to become the next big multi-million dollar as-seen-on-TV product.

CHAPTER 10:

Manufacturing Your Product

"America demands invention and innovation to succeed."

— KIT BOND, AMERICAN POLITICIAN

You have researched your idea, studied your market, sketched your invention, designed your prototype, and planned your commercialization, but the research, planning, and work are still far from done. The physical product is what customers see; it is the representation of everything you have done. Customers must accept your manufactured product, and you need the response and feedback about your product to be positive.

You must first decide how you want your product manufactured, whether you will do everything yourself or form a partnership with a manufacturer. This chapter outlines the manufacturing process and the things to keep in mind about manufacturing.

On Your Own

If you have the means to manufacture your product on your own, this might be the right option for you. This can involve some serious financial commitment, though, so weigh the costs against partnering with a manufacturer. You also need to think about the time commitment involved in manufacturing your own product. Finally, you must know how to make the product.

If you plan to manufacture on your own, you will need to consider all costs involved. Do you have a space where you can produce your invention, either to lease or buy? In addition, if you plan to mass-produce, you must consider the cost of machinery, molds, and people to run the machinery. You will have to pay for utilities and insurance. You also may need to hire additional personnel.

This option might be best for a product you can make quickly and easily. Every inventor has a different product, so there is no obvious choice to always make. For example, if you have a background in carpentry, you might be more able to manufacture a wooden chair than an inventor with a different background. However, most inventors who plan to produce a large quantity of their product get help manufacturing their products.

Doing it yourself: Pros and cons

Making your product yourself is a good choice if you prefer the hands-on approach from start to finish and if you have the resources to do it.

Pros	Cons
Your product will have that personal touch only you can add.	If you get a large order that needs to go out fast, you might not be able to fill it by yourself. You will have to hire help, plus make sure you have enough materials to complete the order. Then you have to train the employees to make it, and take care of quality control before packing and shipping. You must accomplish all this and deliver the order on time or lose a customer, which could lead to negative ratings.
You will know how well the product is made to your specifications during each part of the process.	Even if you have an order form that allows two weeks or more for delivery, you still could lose a customer to a competitor who uses a manufacturer that can fill an order faster.
You are responsible for and in control of every step of the production process, from ordering raw materials to packaging.	You will not get the benefit of your manufacturing company's experience with the industry and the production process.

Even if you make the product yourself, it is still wise to line up a potential manufacturer before you launch, just in case you need a large order. Always be prepared for as many circumstances as possible.

Partnering with a Manufacturer

Finding the right manufacturer involves thorough research and examination. The manufacturer you choose needs to benefit you and your product from the beginning. The ideal manufacturer will want to help protect your interest and will work with you in creating a sustainable partnership. A relationship with a manufacturer is a commitment, just like any other relationship. You must make sure you are compatible, have similar goals and motivations, and can coexist comfortably for a long time.

Choosing a manufacturer: Pros and cons

When you decide to use a manufacturer to create your product, you may choose to have part of your product or the entire design made by the manufacturer. You can negotiate many aspects of the process. The manufacturer can ship the products to you, and you then ship to customers, or it can drop-ship. That means the product moves directly to the retailer without any other distribution channels, so the product goes directly to customers. The manufacturer also may be able to add your product to its retail line and place it onto store shelves. Consider all options as you decide upon the best one that will help your invention be more successful.

Pros	Cons
Mass production — manufacturers already have resources in place to mass-produce many product designs.	When disagreements arise, you must settle them through a negotiation process. For instance, you may have to bend to the manufacturer's processes or pricing if you want your invention out to the mass retail market quickly.
If you are low on capital but your presentation impressed the manufacturer, they will do everything possible to make your invention a quick success.	You are not overseeing every step. You have to depend totally on the manufacturer to make the product meet your specifications and to package and ship it properly. You also have to hope its marketing of your product is successful.
The manufacturer will work with you in every step of the process to make sure your product is up to specifications. You can monitor the entire process if you set up your manufacturing agreement to do so.	You will have to share your profits with the manufacturer.

You have a couple of options for forming a relationship with a manufacturer, each of which is discussed in this section.

Subcontracting

If you want to keep your invention your own but want an outside manufacturer to make your product for you, **subcontracting** is a good option. With this type of arrangement, the manufacturer makes your product, and you pay the manufacturer. You and the manufacturer will work out an agreement describing the arrangement. A lawyer is not necessary to draw up a contract, but one may be able to word it better because he or she will have more experience with this. This agreement should outline details such as the cost to make molds, the cost per unit produced, and time to pay. The more specific you are, the better protected you will be should a cost issue come up during the manufacturing process. If you have everything laid out in the contract, everyone knows what to expect.

With subcontracting, the manufacturer makes money on each unit it produces. You pay for the manufacturer to make the units, and then sell the product on your own. The cost of production will vary depending on the product you are having made. You also may have to pay upfront for special molds or casts to be made for your product.

Joint venture

In a **joint venture** relationship, you enter into an agreement with at least one other party, be it an individual, a group, or a company interested in producing your product. A joint venture divides the expenses and the profits between every investor included in the venture. If the manufacturer sees potential in your invention, it might want to enter into such an arrangement. You share the risk and the rewards, but you also share the control. If you wish to remain completely in charge of your invention, a joint venture might not be right for you.

Manufacturers

You want to find a manufacturer that has experience manufacturing products in the same industry as your invention. If you have prior experience in the industry, you may know the specific manufacturer you want to use. You may also know the method you want to use. However, if you do not have prior experience you will need to do some research.

Manufacturing categories include:

- Casting
- Machining
- Wood working
- Die making
- Textiles
- Electronics
- Stamping
- Fabrication
- Molding
- Mold making
- Assembly
- Engraving
- Extrusion
- Chemical
- Forging

Ways to find a manufacturer:

Plan to find at *least* 20 to 100 manufacturers. Many resources can help you. Start with an Internet search to find companies that make products similar to your invention. For the Burpee Baby Bottle, you would enter "baby bottle" in a search engine such as Google. You also can search online databases, including:

- Thomas Register of Manufacturers Database: Has industrial information, products, services. (**www.thomasnet.com**)
- Harris InfoSource™: Manufacturers by state. (**www.harrisinfo. com/harrisinfo**)
- MacRae's Blue Book: Classic industrial directory. (**www.macraesbluebook.com**)

> MFG Quote: Online quotes for contract manufacturing parts and services. (**www.mfgquote.com**)

> Alibaba® Manufacturing Directory: Extensive directory of manufacturers, suppliers, exporters, and importers. (**www.alibaba. com**)

You can also use resources at your local library such as reference books about different types of manufacturers.

Reviewing manufacturers

There are thousands of manufacturers, and choosing the right one is important. To ensure you are picking the right manufacturer for your invention, learn which criteria to use to judge your choices.

First, find out if the manufacturer is compatible with your product. For instance, a manufacturing company good at making industrial safety supplies probably would be a bad company to choose to make the Burpee Baby Bottle. Ask the manufacturer for information about what types of products it makes. If the manufacturer makes products similar to yours, you know it has the capability to make your product. You can also inspect a product similar to yours that the manufacturer has produced. By looking at past products, you can get an idea of what you can expect from the manufacturer. You also want to choose a manufacturer that will answer questions honestly, has good feedback from others, and is certified.

When choosing a manufacturer for your product, it is important to know how invested the company will be. Companies that are more invested in the products they manufacture tend to produce better results because they have more at stake. For instance, negotiating a higher advancement will mean a more vested company, or choosing a beginner or small company that does not have many other products could be a good idea. A large company tied in with a contract could work, too, though. You must decide the best financial and manufacturing route for you and your invention.

Questioning potential manufacturing companies is crucial. Ask questions about the company, how it does business, and what its procedures are. It is also important to find out how it would produce your invention. Some sample questions include: Does your company charge for samples? What is your smallest batch size? Is packaging included in the unit price? If a company refuses to answer your questions or is evasive in its answers, it is probably a bad company to work with.

Good manufacturing companies will have good references that provide positive feedback. Asking for references will help you choose the best manufacturer for your invention. Investigate the company's background a little. Find out what some of its other customers think of it by checking references with organizations such as the Better Business Bureau® (**www. bbb.org**). Ask around in the local area as well. Chances are if most of the feedback is positive, it is a good company. You can also speak with other inventors who have already had their products manufactured to help you make a good choice. Ask what they liked and disliked about the companies they worked with.

Another defining factor for good manufacturing companies is certification. If the International Organization for Standardization (ISO) certifies the company you are looking at, you can be assured it is a good company with internationally recognized standards of quality. Other companies can certify manufacturers, too, as a way for each business to keep track of the other to ensure quality and safety among business peers. For example, CSA International certifies manufacturers who sell or export to North America. There are also industry-specific certifications, such as the Kitchen Cabinet Manufacturers Association certification. According to the KCMA website, "Cabinets that comply and bear the KCMA Certification Seal are recognized in the marketplace as a quality product able to perform after a rigorous battery of tests simulating years of typical household use." If the manufacturer you are looking at has these certifications, it is likely to be an excellent company. Of course, double-check or verify the certifications in some way.

You also need to make sure the manufacturer you choose can comply with certain terms and standards, such as deadlines, shipping, and quality. These will be important to your product's overall success, and a good manufacturer should be able to assure you they will meet these standards.

Making the Deal

Once you have narrowed down your potential manufacturers, contact each one to set up a meeting. Before this first meeting, you will want to make sure you are protected legally, whether by a patent, trademark, or license agreement. This is a good time to consult an experienced attorney to prepare a nondisclosure agreement. The nondisclosure agreement is a document you will want every serious potential manufacturer to sign before you start disclosing detailed information about your product to them. If the manufacturer refuses to sign the agreement, this is a major red flag, and you need to cease all dealings with this company. Some manufacturers will get the product information from you and produce a similar product to your own. They then become your major competition. Be careful when trying to "sell" your product. Make sure you present your product clearly without divulging too much information. Do your homework, and learn about the manufacturing company before you set the first meeting. Ask for references, and have the nondisclosure agreement signed and returned to you before you take the next step in the process.

Now that you have decided what companies to pitch your product to, you will want to make a clear product presentation. Similar to the presentations you may have given for the licensing, these presentations should result in everyone understanding exactly what your product does. You may want to have a model or prototype of your design to demonstrate what you are talking about. Selling an idea to a manufacturer is a multistep process. You will have to prove your product will fill a need or want with consumers. It may be useful to present a market analysis to prove you have knowledge about consumers. Be ready to give the manufacturer information such as the demographic your product will target and the estimated cost and gross profit of the product. The manufacturer will want to make sure your invention is profitable after the cost of production and will want to know a group of consumers will be willing to pay for your product.

In addition to seeing potential in your product, the manufacturer should meet other certain requirements. For instance, the they should be able to speed your product to market and to keep commitments such as delivery deadlines to retailers. The manufacturer also should be able to guarantee the product's quality. It is crucial that you pair with a manufacturer that can provide certain qualities for you as well. Do not compromise your product. Make sure you hold the manufacturer to high expectations, as they will expect the same from you. Another tip for getting your product manufactured is to realize getting an idea to the store is a process. It will not happen overnight. It is going to take hard work and dedication from everyone involved.

You not only need the manufacturer to trust and believe in your product design, but you also need to make sure you trust the manufacturer. Choosing a manufacturer could be the most crucial business decision you will make regarding your product. It is imperative to your invention's overall success that the relationship between you and the manufacturer is a product-based partnership and that you both have the same goals where the product is concerned. This will ensure everyone's success.

CHAPTER 11:

Traditional Marketing

"I'm an inventor. I became interested in long-term trends because an invention has to make sense in the world in which it is finished, not the world in which it is started."

— RAY KURZWEIL, AMERICAN INVENTOR

An important part of your invention's success is letting the public know about it. Without customers who see the need for your product — and who will spend their money on it — you will not be successful. **Marketing** is the way you go about letting potential customers know about your products or services and how those products or services satisfy and meet their needs. There are thousands of approaches and strategies for marketing, but they all are aimed at the same goal: to influence people to try or continue to use your product.

If you have decided to start a business based around your invention, marketing strategies and efforts will be especially paramount to your ultimate success. The success of your invention and the payoff for all the time and money you have invested to get to this point rely on this next step: marketing. Some experts believe you should spend $10 in marketing for every $1 you spend in product development, according to marketing ratios. The best form of marketing is one that remains creative, remains profitable for everyone, and builds on relationships. When you focus on people, not dollar signs, your venture will grow through integrity and good relations with customers.

Create your marketing plan and review it at least once a year. Marketing efforts are ever-changing and growing, adapting to the market, the product, and the climate of the sales environment. Your goal is to always have satisfied customers who return and bring more customers with them. Word-of-mouth marketing among your clients can mean big business for you; satisfying one customer can result in ten new customers coming your way.

Branding Your Product

When walking down the aisle at the grocery store, you can likely identify your favorite products without even reading the words on the label. You can identify the colors, the fonts, the shapes, and the size. Your favorite soda might be in a bright red carton with white letters. Your favorite macaroni and cheese might be in a rectangular blue box, which even began a marketing campaign in the 1990s featuring "The Blue Box" and commercials about children having "the blues."

A **brand** is what identifies a product (or company). According to the American Marketing Association, a brand is "a name, term, sign, symbol, or design, or a combination which is intended to identify the goods or services of one seller or a group of sellers and to differentiate them from those of competitors." Your brand should not only show your product is different and distinguish your product from competitors', but it should signal your brand is better.

Define your brand before your product is marketed. Here are some things to think about when deciding on your branding strategy:

> **Your product:** Why did you invent the product? What purpose does it fill? What emotions does it elicit?

> **Your market:** Who are you selling to? What types of consumers will use your product? What are the values of the customers in your market?

Your Target Market

One of the first things you need to do is pinpoint your target market. A **target market** is the demographic you wish to reach with your marketing plan, or, simply, the group of people whom your invention appeals to the most. A **demographic group** may be categorized by age, gender, race, culture, region, education, occupation, or hobby, or a combination of any of these factors. There are two main reasons you want to focus your efforts in the beginning on a target market: 1) By marketing your product to everyone, you will actually market it to no one, and a focused strategy will be the most cost-effective marketing strategy. 2) Instead of doing a blanket marketing campaign — just trying to get anyone with a heartbeat to buy your product — you will be directing your efforts to the consumers most likely to buy your product.

The demographic for some inventions may be easy to recognize. For example, a highly technical invention made for the medical field will be marketed exclusively to medical professionals and businesses. Other inventions, such as household appliances, might require more market research, such as statistical evaluation and market surveys, to identify the strongest audience.

To identify your target market, first determine a specific geographic area or areas to begin the marketing process. You may have to start small, such as a county or state, or even in a retailer that is only in a certain region of the country. Based on what you know about your client base, look at demographics of different regions to choose the one where your product will be the most successful. For instance, a tractor part may not sell well in New York City, but it may do great in Georgia. You also can target a specific type of customer who will be most likely to buy your product. For example, if you are selling an organizer for a college dorm room, you would want to target college students or soon-to-be college students, as well as the parents of those students. Concentrate your marketing efforts on these people.

Logos

Your **logo** is the visual representation of your company, product, or brand. A brand is a name, whereas a logo would be a certain display of your name or an image associated with your brand. It should be unique and memorable because its main purpose is recognition. Images, words, shapes, colors, layout, and spatial aspects are joined to form a unique logo. Once customers see your logo enough, they will start to immediately associate it with your brand. This increases brand recognition and equity.

Your logo will be used not only on the product itself, but also on the packaging, marketing materials, web copy, and more. Your logo is what identifies your product.

Logo design

If you have experience with graphic design you can consider designing your own logo. If you have minimal to no experience with graphic design, it is best to turn to a professional to design your logo. There are several free logo makers online, but the resulting logos from these sites are unprofessional and not unique.

Professional logo designers will interview you about your product and research the industry to see what types of logos competitors use. They also look at what designs have been successful in the given industry. They then go through several stages of design and feedback, usually designing multiple variations of a logo.

Logo design tips

> Be sure your logo looks professional. Your logo represents your company and product. Potential customers may be turned off and think your company or product is substandard if your logo looks unprofessional.

> Do not use stock art in your logo. This looks unprofessional and can also be a violation of copyright laws. Your logo needs to be a unique image.

> ➤ Do not use more than two font styles in your logo. Using more than two fonts can be confusing and turn off potential customers. Using fewer font styles also improves brand recognition.

> ➤ Do not copy another logo. This should go without saying, but taking the image of another logo is illegal.

Successfully Marketing Your Invention

The market for your invention is one of the factors in determining its price. If you are marketing toward a small, specific population and your product is totally unique, advanced, or significantly better than a similar product, you may be able to charge a higher price. On the other hand, if you are marketing toward a broader population and your product has a good deal of competition or is simple, charge a lower price to remain competitive.

Having determined a demographic and product price, you are ready to start promoting your invention. Your marketing options are as broad as your imagination. If your marketing fund is scant, you might choose to start small and market your invention yourself. The cheapest form of advertising is word-of-mouth. To reach a larger audience, consider advertising in the local newspaper or buying a small spot on the radio. The Internet is a fantastic venue for reaching a large audience and offers many cost-effective marketing solutions. *See Chapter 13 for more on Internet marketing.* You also might choose to rent a booth at public consumer events such as swap meets or trade shows. Remember that self-marketing may be cheaper, but it should not look cheaper. Companies such as FedEx Office can provide you with professional-looking promotional materials. Demonstrations are also a good way to show the value of your invention.

If you are working on a larger scale, a variety of professionals are available to provide services proven to have effective results. You can consult with marketing firms, advertising firms, designers, and packaging experts to ensure your marketing is perfectly planned down to the last detail. Many companies offer Web conferences, or Webinars, to talk about marketing techniques. Although expensive, the resources and expertise these companies bring to your project may make sure your invention has immediate status in the marketplace, which will put you on the fast track toward success.

With the right marketing, even inventors who start small have the potential for big success.

Trade shows

Trade shows are one of the most important events to attend to gain a market for your product, says Dr. Pamela Riddle Bird. A trade show is an event held in a location, such as a convention center, where manufacturers and marketers can display their products and technologies to potential buyers, retailers, wholesalers, and others in their industry.

Trade shows offer huge opportunities. As the saying goes, it is not about what you know; rather, it is all about *who* you know. Attending trade shows allows you to meet people in your industry. Networking with people in your industry provides opportunities. This, coupled with a useful product, can be the jumping point you need for success. At a trade show, you get to know people face-to-face instead of tracking them down by calling or e-mailing them.

At a trade show, you can set up a booth to display your invention. Bird says this is a necessary expense, as it gives small companies or new inventors a level playing field with the major players in the industry. The cost of a booth can be several thousand dollars.

To find trade shows, check the *Encyclopedia of Associations*. Here are some examples:

> INPEX® - Invention & New Product Exposition
  www.inpex.com

> IENA - Ideas, Inventions, New Products Exhibition
  www.iena.de/en/home.html

> The Australian Innovation Festival
  www.ausinnovation.org

> International Fair for Invention
  http://www.mtgsa.com.pl/title,lang,2.html

> Brussels Eureka!
  www.brussels-eureka.be

> Taipei International Invention Show & Technomart
  www.inventaipei.com.tw

> The Ultimate Trade Show Directory
  www.tsnn.com

Developing a Marketing Plan

At times, it can be difficult to implement marketing techniques that actually work. People who have never been trained or educated in the fine points of marketing may understand how marketing works because of their personal experiences. Experience has taught them what works, and they have built on the foundation of customer satisfaction.

Taking a practical approach to marketing means setting daily, weekly, monthly, and yearly marketing goals. Whether at the point of sale or through the form of e-mails or direct marketing pieces, implement something marketing-related daily. This also could include network-marketing breakfasts, lunches, and dinners; carrying business cards everywhere and passing them out when appropriate; and using promotional items such as bumper stickers and pens to spread the word.

Staying in contact with your customers is an important channel for communicating new marketing strategies. Newsletters, websites, blogs, and social media sites such as Facebook and Twitter allow you to be in personal contact with your target audience. With these tools, you can share new promotions, gather market research, take surveys, learn opinions, and introduce new products or service changes. You also can send out reminders and share new technology.

What is a marketing plan?

If you are in the process of launching a new invention, product, brand, service, or concept, having a thorough marketing plan is necessary to attaining your goals. A **marketing plan** is a written document that details the various, interdependent actions necessary to enable you to achieve one or more of your marketing objectives.

A marketing plan's duration is often for one year, though it can vary from company to company. For instance, the plan can be either short-term (quarterly) or long-term (more than one year). Although the marketing plan is a mandatory component of the overall business plan, it must evolve from another critical process to succeed. To prepare a professional, realistic marketing plan, it is imperative for you to carry out a comprehensive, in-depth marketing audit of the inputs provided by various in-house departments throughout the year. You can hire a qualified, external source to do this, particularly if you do not possess a specialized department to do so. Again, strategic planning can be carried out for just the immediate year ahead or, if found feasible, for a longer period (three years or more).

The marketing strategy

The first step in your marketing plan is to define your **marketing strategy**, your detailed plan for using limited resources to obtain the greatest results in terms of sales and competitive advantage in the marketplace. Even good inventions may fail commercially without a good marketing strategy. Your strategy should combine the following four components, known as the **marketing mix variables** and often called the four Ps:

> **Product:** The invention itself

> **Promotion:** Communication, advertising, and other methods of letting the public know about your product

> **Place (or distribution):** How you will get the product into consumers' hands

> **Price:** How much you will charge for your product, including discounts, financing options, and leasing options

Product

The first P is the **product** itself. This includes the tangible product as well as the name of it, its design/style, its quality, warranty or guarantees, and accessories. It is also how the product looks, including its packaging.

You may think of packaging as just something to hold your product. Thinking this way will greatly limit your product's ability to market itself. Before you approach any big retail chain or broker, it is important to have a product and package that is attractive and presented in an appealing manner. Anything less already stands a chance of rejection. To be on the shelves next to already established products, you have to actively compete for a consumer's attention. Therefore, packaging is everything. Many businesses realize that a big portion of their budgets will go toward the packaging of their products. Image sells, so package your products to compete.

Considering how many different products are available and how they are all trying to get potential buyers to look at them through the use of unique packaging, it is vital that your invention is packaged to sell. If you do proper research and proactively pursue good packaging for your invention, the rewards will be high.

The first thing to realize when considering packaging is you have to research types. You can do this in many different ways, and few methods require large sums of money. The easiest way to research packaging is to visit stores that sell similar products to yours. If your invention is a unique idea, then visit stores that sell other unique products. Another research method is to visit trade shows and see how new products are packaged there. One of the more expensive ways to research packaging is to subscribe to publications in your product's field, as well as publications specifically related to packaging. Ask yourself a few questions when researching packaging:

> What size and shape should the package be? How will it be displayed? If it will be sitting on a shelf, will the packages stack?

> What colors would be appealing to consumers? Look at the colors used; which will work for you?

> Will my product need to be protected with sturdy packaging? If so, will the packaging protect the product?

Packaging for your invention should be eye-catching and informative. It should tell potential buyers everything they need to know about your product. If a potential buyer does not know the purpose of a product, they will not purchase it. The packaging is the first thing the consumer sees and needs to draw in the consumer without causing confusion.

Other great sources for input concerning packaging information are friends, family, fellow inventors, and your manufacturer. The people around you can be useful resources. They may have a new angle on your invention you never considered before. Your manufacturer will have good ideas on how to package your product from a business standpoint, and friends and family will have good ideas about how to package based on a consumer standpoint.

While choosing packaging for your product, also consider your target audience and how many products you will make. If your target market is large, the packaging should be more versatile so you can market to and reach a wider audience. The package depends entirely upon the product and its target market. If your target audience consists of older women, the packaging would look completely different than if your target audience were young children. A child is more likely to choose a package with bright colors, pictures, and few words. Older women will be drawn to softer hues and text. For the Burpee Baby Bottle, the packaging should be geared toward mothers, with cute designs and appealing, kid-friendly images. Pictures of happy babies, cartoon animal babies, or cartoon babies with the Burpee Baby Bottle in their hands could work.

Promotion

Promotion includes the advertising and public relations aspect of marketing. It is critical with promotion to reach your particular population of customers. Your goal with promotion is to provide your message about your product to the people who are most likely to buy it. Choose avenues of advertisement directed at your potential customer base. For example, with the Burpee Baby Bottle, you need your messages to be heard by parents, soon-to-be parents, or other people who might be thinking about having a baby soon. Placing an advertisement in *Hunting Magazine* would likely not return much in the way of results.

Place

Once you get your product manufactured, you have to secure means for distributing it. There are several options for **places** or ways to sell your product. Specifically, you can opt for direct or indirect sales. **Direct sales** involve you selling directly to the end customer, whereas **indirect sales** involve a middleman, you sell your product to someone else to distribute to the customer. Consequently, the price goes up.

For example, you can decide to sell your product through stores. This can be through direct sales in your own stores or indirect sales through retail chains. You can sell through websites — your own and others, such as

Amazon.com. Infomercials, direct mail (catalogs/flyers), or direct sales (home/catalog parties) are also options for selling your invention.

Store

If you do not buy or rent your own space for a store, you will need to decide what stores in which your product fits best. A few types of stores to consider are specialty stores, a big box store, a high-end store, a discount market, a local store, or a national chain. To get your product into these retailers, you need to contact their corporate offices.

Website

Selling through a website can entail either creating your own your site and selling your product or selling your product through someone else's site. These are not mutually exclusive, and you may decide you want to sell through multiple outlets. Having your own website for your invention is a must to survive in the current marketplace. However, whether you actually sell your product through your website is your choice. *Learn more about creating a website in Chapter 12.*

If you decide not to sell your invention on your website or if you also want to create more opportunities for sales, you can try to sell it on other sites. There are specialized online-only retailers that sell almost everything you can imagine. For example, there are sites dedicated to animals and animal products, products for the elderly, toys, and household gadgets. The website **www.catalogs.com** can help you find online retailers of products similar to your invention.

Mail-order catalogs

Mail-order catalogs are a form of indirect sales and are an option for selling your product. Inventions that are now common household items were introduced to the market through mail-order catalogs. For example, in 1930 Hammacher Schlemmer introduced the pop-up toaster through its mail-order catalog. The majority of mail-order companies buy products and re-sell them to consumers. According to the National Mail Order Association, mail-order catalogs comprise a $400 billion industry in the United States and Canada, and there are over 12,000 mail-order catalogs in the same area. Some examples of the larger mail-order catalogs include Lillian Vernon, Johnson-Smith, Brookstone, Hanover House, Sharper Image, and Fingerhut. These catalogs mail millions of copies to subscribers.

There are a few resources you can use to find mail-order companies. The first is Grey House Publishing's Directory of Mail-Order Catalogs, which lists 10,000 mail-order companies in the U.S. The directory is organized by industry. You can order directly from Grey House's website (**www. greyhouse.com**). The cost as of 2010 is $395 plus shipping. You can also likely find this in the reference section of your local library.

Another resource is Oxbridge Communications' National Directory of Catalogs, which includes more than 12,000 catalogs in North America. The cost for the 2009 National Directory of Catalogs is $995. You can order via Oxbridge's website (**www.oxbridge.com/NDCCluster/theNDC.asp**).

Oxbridge also maintains the MediaFinder Catalog Search. The search is available online (**https://secured.mediafinder.com/secure/secure. cfm?page=NMOA/CatalogSearchForm**). Using this site, you can search by category for online and print catalogs. The site also tells you how many results match your search. For example, for our Burpee Baby Bottle, the search would be for "Baby/Pregnancy." Leaving the other search options open (e.g., online and print, all locations, etc.), there are 57 matches. As of 2010, the fee is $0.20 per result with a minimum charge of $50. Along with the name of each catalog, you get the name of the company that publishes the catalog, the address, country, phone, fax, website address, media type, and target audience.

The National Mail Order Association also maintains a database of inventions for catalog companies to find. An inventor pays a fee of $99 for three months to have an invention listed in the database as well sent in the e-mailed newsletter to their members (which includes 8,000 catalogs).

Price

Price in the marketing mix not only includes the retail price, but also the pricing for wholesale/bulk purchases, bundling, financing options, and discounts/sales.

Setting the price for your product is one of the most crucial factors in determining whether people buy your invention. You may have created a well-made product with a noticeable label. Consumers may even see the necessity and usefulness of your invention. But if your price is too high, consumers will not buy the product. If your price is too low, you will lose profits and may not be able to cover your costs. Coming up with a reasonable product price is essential for the life of your invention.

You also need to pay attention to the economy. Is your product elastic, meaning that if the price changes, the demand changes with it? For example, in a good economy, consumers may find your product, the Burpee Baby Bottle, a nice luxury they will pay $3 more than a regular bottle to have. However, if you keep your price $3 above average in a bad economy, your demand will most likely fall. Parents will start burping their babies on their own instead. However, if you invent a cure for diabetes, those who suffer the disease will most likely pay high costs no matter what the economy is like because it affects their way of life. This would be an inelastic product. Gasoline and electricity are other examples of inelastic products, while hair products and clothing are elastic.

Calculating your costs

To know how much to charge for each unit, you first need to calculate how much you will spend on each unit. Determining what expenses you have going out will help you set an accurate price so you are making the money needed to cover the cost of each unit, plus profit. You might have thought through what it will cost to produce your inventions; however, you have likely underestimated the costs. In addition to the materials to be included in the invention, there are other things to consider. It will also help you establish to a price range for what you should charge for your product though there are other expenses you have to take into consideration when determining the retail price of the product.

You have two types of costs: fixed costs and variable costs. The **fixed costs** are costs that will stay the same no matter how many items you make or order. Examples of fixed costs include product molds, tools, and equipment. On the other hand, **variable costs** can vary based on a number of reasons, including the number of units produced/ordered or market value. When you order more of a material or product, the cost per unit generally goes down. However, you do not want to order too many units and have unsold products. It is ideal for your supply to be even with your demand, not greater than your demand.

The costs of the materials to make your product add up quickly. These includes raw materials, individual parts or components, any type of adhesive or fastener, and anything else that goes into making your product. You likely will buy your components in quantities for mass production, so calculate the cost of each component necessary for one unit of your invention. Add up the components to get the total cost of materials for one unit.

Producing the product yourself

To determine the prices of the materials, you first need to make a list of the materials you need. This will include not only parts and pieces, but also the cost of other items, such as paints, screws, adhesive, and molds.

Many business people look at costs in terms of **mills**, which is a tenth of a cent. Using mills instead of cents gives you a better idea of your actual costs. For example, if you have a product that is going to cost 15 cents to manufacture, it will cost you $1,500 to manufacture 10,000 ($0.15 x 10,000=$1,500). However, when you price it out in mills, you find out that each one is going to cost $0.156 to make, which means your 10,000 products are now going to cost $1,560 ($0.156 x 10,000=$1,560). Sixty dollars might not sound like a lot, but over time when you begin ordering more and more product, this really adds up. So when you calculate the cost of materials and other things associated with the production costs, ask for costs in mills.

> **Production:** If you are having a company manufacture your product, you need to calculate the cost of having each unit made. If you are producing the product yourself, consider the costs of machines, materials, facilities/offices, and utilities.

> **Packaging:** This is sometimes an overlooked aspect of calculating costs. The cost of packaging might seem minimal, especially in comparison to the cost of materials and production. However, even a few pennies per package make a huge difference when calculating in thousands or millions of units. Do not forget to calculate the cost of packaging materials and equipment.

> **Sales:** Unless you are willing to attract every buyer yourself, you will have to hire a salesperson to sell the products for you. Most salespeople work on commission. A good starting point is to figure a 20 percent commission per unit sold.

> **Shipping:** The cost of shipping depends on the weight of the product, its packaging to keep it safe during transportation, the size of the package, and its destination. Generally, the farther it is going, the more it costs; however, there are flat rates for certain weights within the United States. Also, figure in any packing materials such as boxes, tape, and bubble wrap or peanuts.

> **Other costs:** As if all the above costs were not enough, you have to consider other expenses associated with your invention. These include graphic design, office supplies, administrative workers and other employees, marketing materials, advertising, and consulting. Figure that 10 percent of the cost of your product will go toward these expenses. Marketing and advertising should be the most expensive part of your model, as explained with the "10:1" ratio used earlier.

Setting a price

The price of your product is another major decision for your invention. Determining your costs is the first step in setting the price. Your market price should cover your manufacturing, shipping, and marketing costs, while still allowing you to make a profit (eventually) and compete with similar products.

You do want your price to be competitive, however. If you set your price too high, you may not sell as many units as you would have if your prices had been closer to competitors' prices. On the other hand, if you set your price too low, consumers may think your product is "cheap," which may turn some people off. Decide what is right for your invention based on what you envision for your product. Determine where you plan to sell your product when deciding the pricing.

The Components of a Great Marketing Plan

You are thinking about selling your product, and you realize you need a marketing plan. All great marketing plans have these components: goals, target audiences, budgets, and research. If you incorporate these elements, you will likely have a good plan, and your product will sell well.

The first component to a good marketing plan is goals. It is important to know what you want the marketing plan to do. If you are hoping to sell globally one day, then your goals need to reflect that. If you want people to become more aware of your product as a whole, then your goals will be different. Plan your goals carefully because an unclear goal will produce unclear results. Your goal must define exactly what you want to accomplish from your product.

The next component of a good marketing plan is determining the demographics of your target audience. Determine who you want buying your product, be it baby boomers, small children, or teens. It is important that you identify the target audience for your marketing strategy. Blanket marketing with no specific audience will get you no results. Also, regardless of who you think will use the product, the target audience should always be the audience with the largest buying power or the group with the most flexible income. In many cases, the person with the most buying power is not the person who will use the product. For example, parents will be doing the purchasing for children's products, so you need to include them in your marketing plan as well. With the Burpee Baby Bottle, the babies will not be purchasing it; rather, the parents will do so. The market needs to appeal to them instead. Also, remember that if you are marketing to children, your strategy will be vastly different than a strategy that markets to wealthy, retired people. Each target audience will need a different marketing strategy.

Once you have identified your target audience, the next component in creating a good marketing plan is having a firm budget. Determine how much you are willing to spend on your goals and, more importantly, how much the benefits you hope to gain are worth. If you can afford it, a larger budget usually produces larger results. If your invention is going to be sold on a smaller scale, it is probably best to keep costs low. Spending too much on a marketing plan could spell disaster for smaller companies. You must spend money wisely in the beginning to realize any profit. Whatever the budget, it is vital that you stick to it. Many companies have failed because they did not stick to their budgets.

The last step in forming a good marketing strategy is proper research. Now that you know what you want to do and for whom, it is time to find out what marketing techniques get them to purchase the most. There are many ways to do this, ranging from going to the kinds of stores that your target audience frequents to having market research conducted specifically for your product. The method you choose does not really matter as long as it fits the scale of your goal and your budget. The more involved your research is, however, the more effectively you will be able to reach your goals. So even if you have little money to spend, be sure your research is thorough.

After following these steps, you have created a great marketing plan. All that is left is acting on your plan. Now is the time to fulfill your goals by implementing your strategy and increasing your business. Any good marketing plan will increase sales of your invention. Marketing success relies on the efforts you put into your marketing plan. If you are really serious about selling your product, spend plenty of time on your marketing plan. The biggest mistake you can make in creating your marketing plan is thinking it is not important. Your marketing plan is almost as important as the invention itself.

Getting the Word Out

Along with your sound marketing plan, have a plan for public relations. A basic definition of **public relations** is managing the relationship between your company and the public. It involves media relations, promotions, customer relations, and special event planning, with the ultimate goal of maintaining or improving the perception of your company and product or protecting and maintaining your reputation.

A major facet of public relations is media relations. One goal for marketing and promotion is to get stories and coverage about your company or product in various media outlets. This form of promotion is free and could reach a new audience.

Start by creating a **press kit**, or **media kit**. This is a prepackaged bundle of promotional materials such as pamphlets, reviews, photos, and background information to hand out to clients. This kit will help inform reporters about your product, company, or any newsworthy events or other things associated with your company or product. Your press kit will help a reporter write the best story possible about your company or invention. Although you can hire someone to put this together, you can also make your own to save money. In a pocket folder, include your company brochure, a short bio of yourself and any company officers, any press releases or articles about the company or product, and a letter explaining what is included in the kit, along with contact information. Include business cards and novelty items such as magnets or pens personalized with your company logo. Keep extra press kits at your office and pass them out at community events and trade shows. You never know when you might meet a potential customer.

You can use a variety of free or low-cost ways to market your product. If your local radio station has a call-in show, use it to help plug your product. Most radio, television, and newspaper offices have e-mail addresses listed on their websites. E-mail your information to anyone who might help plug your product. Anywhere you can get your information to the public is a plus.

Consumers like to feel they are getting good prices for products. Consider offering discounts for people willing to buy in bulk. Customers also love to enter contests. You could give away a gift or gift certificate after you reach a specific number of visits to your website or make a certain number of sales. For example, you can give a $25 gift certificate to the 100th person who buys your product.

Go to as many trade shows as possible so you can exhibit or demonstrate your product in person. Have brochures on hand to pass out. If you have time, flea markets and festivals are also a good way to begin getting your product into the public eye. People at these events always love finding new things and getting bargains. Have business cards on hand to pass out, too.

You can also go to the companies that you buy products or services from and talk to them about your invention. Give them a brochure and business card. Ask whether they or anyone they know could use your product. If they allow business cards to be displayed, be sure to put yours up.

To bring exposure to your product, begin by attending the meetings of different professional groups, such as Rotary clubs or civic organizations. Try to be as involved as possible in a few groups, and remember to pass out your business cards as often as you can. Send out flyers or brochures in a direct mail campaign, where you send information directly to potential consumers. Send them to everyone in your address book. Sites on the Internet sell or trade mailing lists for these purposes, such as Direct Mail (**www.directmail.com**). Ask friends and family to help distribute your information. You can leave flyers under windshield wipers at shopping malls, restaurants, or sporting events. As a last resort, you can pull addresses from your local phone book (online or print) to circulate your brochure even farther.

Never forget word-of-mouth referrals. Have your friends and family mention your product to as many people as possible. Some consumers buy products based on personal referrals. You may consider giving several products as gifts to people close to you so they have firsthand knowledge of the product and can show it if the opportunity arises. Do not forget to use your vehicle as a marketing tool. Have a magnetic sign made to market your product or website. This way, you can remove it when needed or advertise wherever you go.

CHAPTER 12

Marketing via the Internet

"Interest is the spur of the people, but glory that of great souls. Invention is the talent of youth, and judgment of age."

— JONATHAN SWIFT

If you ran a small business ten or 15 years ago and you wanted to promote yourself, you relied on costly printed advertisements such as brochures or flyers, you ran expensive ads on radio or television, or you depended strongly on word of mouth. In today's rapidly growing, ever-changing technological world, the Internet and e-mail have changed the way to market and promote your business. Companies no longer have to depend on word-of-mouth and persuasive print ads because of online advertising. Use of the Internet means you can directly reach your target market. **Internet marketing** is an affordable solution to expensive marketing strategies, and it reaches many more people — but you must know the right steps to get your message out there.

Another big advantage of advertising online is that, on the Internet, nobody knows the size of your business or company. Ten years ago, you may have been at a disadvantage just starting out because people would tend to be skeptical of buying a product from a business that was not established. The only way to establish a business is through sales. These facts created a dilemma for businesses trying to get off the ground. Today, by advertising online, potential clients or customers will not know whether you are an established business or are completely new, depending on your advertising techniques and strategies, thus giving you an advantage as a "salesperson."

Marketing via the Internet also allows you to become successful at selling your product or business because you always have a "fresh crop" of clients available. For example, once you become successful in your hometown, your business might grow quickly because of word-of-mouth, or your sales may stall for a while because the community has already been exposed to your product. With Internet marketing, you can reach a wide range of people. This means your product will always be new to someone. Internet marketing makes you better equipped to see which marketing strategies are working and which are not because you get faster results. Free tools like Google Analytics™ can help you see who is viewing your site and where they are from, as well as how much time they spend there.

If your product is doing well in stores, the Internet will help you extend your reach to make even more money. You can set up many online avenues of free marketing for your successful retail product. All the product information you place on the Web will be seen by potentially billions of people all over the world and also can stay online for years. These are good reasons to include the Internet when marketing your invention. Also, with the Internet now accessible on cell phones, sales potential is increased even more as consumers come across your product on their phone via your website or online advertisement. A company can even advertise their products in applications for smart phones. New Internet-related technologies for communicating will provide even more avenues of future potential sales success for years to come.

Even when your product is located in a national chain store on the market, additional online exposure will increase sales potential. The more potential customers who see your product repeatedly, the more it becomes closer to becoming a "household name." All the positive feedback you receive helps create what is known as **viral marketing** online. This technique uses pre-established social networking sites to increase awareness. Viral marketing was well known for decades offline as "word-of-mouth marketing." Customers use the Internet to research products, and having positive comments about your product from customers is the best marketing. On the Internet, you receive the added benefit of these comments staying online for years. When people write the name of your product when making positive comments about it, those comments will show up in major search engines such as Google and Yahoo!, and other potential buyers will find them. This is a big advantage to your sales potential, and it is all free advertising from your customers.

Of course, it is important to understand that the same can be true for any negative comments about your product. This is why you want to work on positive interactions with all potential customers at all times, online as well as offline. Consumers will judge how you reply to negative comments, and their perceptions will contribute to increased or decreased sales over a long period of time. Your replies to negative comments also remain online for years. Remember to choose your words carefully when responding to any negative public relations online.

Inventors today have new ways to advertise products to the masses that cost them millions less than their predecessors. The Internet is reshaping marketing into a whole new medium on a global scale and is doing it much quicker than anyone ever imagined. Take advantage of the opportunity to further your success by potentially millions of sales for years to come. It might not have occurred without the Internet, especially not for free or at an exceptionally lower cost than any time in marketing history.

Internet marketing has become one of the biggest industries in the world. Just about every business has a presence on the Internet, and if they do not, they soon will. Ways to market online include finding targeted newsgroups and automated e-mail lists where you can form relationships. Join forums, write blogs and articles, and promote yourself as an expert in your field. Educate, inform, and exchange knowledge with your audiences online. Search engine optimization (SEO) — writing content for your website using keywords that will put you at the top of search engine results — should become a marketing technique you perfect.

Think marketing all day long, from how you answer your phone when customers call to your answering-machine message after hours. Consider simple marketing techniques you may have overlooked. For example, use your e-mail signature to promote your products, services, and website. As marketing becomes a more crucial part of your business plan, it will give life to all you do from start to finish, in your work and in your relationships with customers.

The Correct Steps to Market Your Product Online

If you are ready to market your product online, here are some tips to get you started. Be prepared to put some time and effort into your project to make it successful. Once you get your own website set up, you will have several marketing options.

Affiliate programs

Try **affiliate programs**, which allow other people to sell your product through their websites or newsletters. You can find affiliates by looking at clubs or associations that may be interested in your product. They can put a link on their site to go to a separate website to buy your product. By giving affiliates a special URL, or Web address, you can track which sites your visitors come from. Discuss ahead of time whether these sites will get a small fee when someone purchases your product through them or whether this is a free service. Participation in affiliate programs can help get attention for your site. Also, you can link your site to other sites, usually for free. This will help drive traffic to you and to the site hosting your link. When someone clicks on your link, it takes him or her directly to your site. Anywhere you can get your Web address seen will help bring traffic to you.

Pay-per-click advertising

Test your new product using **pay-per-click advertising**. This is an Internet advertising model used on websites, in which advertisers (you) pay their host (the website) only when their ad is clicked. Choose a list of keywords describing your product. Then, when someone clicks on your ad and visits your site, you pay a fee. If budget is a concern, however, think seriously about whether you can afford this before signing up for a service. Costs can vary, but, for instance, Google AdWords™ charges $5 per day and 10 cents every time the banner or ad is clicked on. Be sure to research the company you do the pay-per-click advertising with, and double-check before paying. You also can design professional-quality banner ads to use on your website, banner exchange sites, or paid advertising campaigns. Banner ads are the rectangular boxes that often appear at the top, bottom, and sides of websites. Several sites can help you design a banner for free or at a small cost. These ads keep your product in the public eye and help with memory recall when consumers see them at a later date.

Press release distribution

Free and paid **press release syndication** services can give your site more visibility and keep marketing costs as low as possible. A search online for "press release syndication" will turn up plenty of options. Distributing your information through these services sends news about your product to different newspapers and media hubs throughout the United States, and they help customers learn more about you and your product. Similarly, article distribution to webmasters and publishers can get your product name to a variety of customers. Sites such as Ezine (**www.ezinearticles. com**) run this service. Then there are **target text ads**, which show up on searches and on the sides of some sites. These ads should be well written and specific, but take care to keep them short and simple. The ad headline should contain your best keywords. Below the headline, describe your product and list its benefits. Always make sure the correct Web address is listed. Also, it is best to have several ads for each group of your market.

Forums

Join **forums** such as Yahoo! Groups® to gain visibility. These are discussion sites or message boards. This makes it easier for people to find your site and subscribe to your newsletter, if you have one. It also helps generate word-of-mouth advertising. Enlist a friend to go in some online chat rooms with you. You can have a discussion about your product and website. Other people who see this may follow your link to look around and return when they are ready to make a purchase. Be sure all your correspondence, including personal e-mails, has your website clearly listed. Even if people do not visit your site right away, the name will be familiar when they see it later, and this helps bring in customers when they are ready to buy, which is called brand awareness. Post your website link on any online advertising sites and message boards you can find. Some businesses that have websites offer online bulletin boards for business cards. Display yours on as many as possible.

Major search engines

Another important Internet marketing strategy is gaining the attention of the major search engines. This will do wonders for your advertising and the effect it has on your small business. Keep in mind when setting up your business website what the search engines look for when ranking sites. The sites consider two main elements. One is how unique and relevant the site's content is as well as how fresh it is by tracking how often content is updated. Change the information frequently and keep it new. The other element is how many incoming links you have from other sites, preferably high-ranked ones. Here is where you need to add links to your website, help promote other sites, and have those sites link to your site. Simply head a section as "useful links" or "helpful links" and list some relevant websites.

These tips will not only help with search engine promotion, but they are also good advertising and marketing strategies in themselves. The more places your business is visible, the more people, and potential customers, you will reach.

Start an online store

Running an online store will also increase the sales of your product. You can add a newsletter to the store to discuss more about the product and ask for feedback from customers who use it. Make sure to let them know their feedback will be posted on your website. You can have the feedback rotate as customers add new comments. When you run a professional online store, your sales potential will increase because of the additional exposure of your product, plus the convenience for customers to have it shipped to them. You also can include an option for customers to order online and then pick up the product at a store in their area, or just research whether the product is in a local store.

Many online marketing avenues are available for free, including blogs, forums, social networking, podcasts, and video broadcasting, with more outlets appearing daily. The advantage of using these networks to market your product occurs when these sites constantly rotate your product information among everyone else's on the site. Your advertisement is not left stagnant, waiting for you to promote it. The advertisers on these sites do not have to worry about marketing their information. That is the beauty of becoming a member when you want to maximize your product's brand name and exposure quickly. The more you place new content in any site you are a member of, the more it is rotated as the latest blog, latest forum discussion, or latest profile change.

Just remember that any visibility you can get for your website and your product will help keep it in customer's minds when they are ready to buy. Even if they do not buy the first time they visit your site, by keeping your product in the public eye, you will give them a familiar name when they are ready.

Creating a website

If you are like many consumers in this technology age, the Internet is one of the first places you go when trying to find something. Whether it is an address or phone number of a business or customer reviews of a certain product, the Internet is a great resource for finding information. Having a website to highlight your invention will be the easiest way for potential customers to find your product.

Even people with no prior web design experience can create a website. If you can afford the cost, you can also hire someone to do it for you. The first steps involved are the same regardless of whether you do it yourself or hire someone else. Here are some things to think about in regard to your website:

> ➢ **Your domain name (the URL people type in to go to your site):** The tricky part to this is finding a unique domain. It should be short and easy to remember. It must also still be available. If the name of your invention is unique, that may be a good choice for your domain (just add the .com to the end). You can check availability of domains at **www.register.com** or **www.godaddy.com**. If your domain is still available, you can purchase it through those sites.

> ➢ **Your site visitors:** You might not think your audience is important and that you just need to get the site up. Remember, it is always

important to remember your audience. For example, if your product is targeted toward a younger audience, it needs to be flashier and more interactive than a product designed for older generations. To illustrate this, look at the website for Mountain Dew (**www.mountaindew.com**) and compare that with the site for Citracal (**www.citracal.com**). It is evident that the site for Mountain Dew is targeted at a younger generation, whereas the Citrical is targeted at an older age group.

➤ **Message:** If your invention is a higher end product, your website should illustrate that. If it is whimsical, your site should convey that. In short, your site should reflect your product and company.

➤ **Components of the site:** Websites can include a number of different components, including forums, blogs, games, and shopping. Do you want to give your customers the ability to order directly from your site? If not, do you want them to be able to request a catalog from you or call an 800 number to order? If you are not offering the product for purchase on your site and it is strictly informational, how will you let customers know where to purchase your product?

One of the best ways to determine what components you want on your site is to visit other websites. Make a list of the features you like and what would work for your site/invention. Do not forget to keep your audience in mind.

➤ **Launching the site:** Consider the optimal time to start your website. Do you want to inform customers about your product when you are still in the commercialization phase or do you want to wait until manufacturing is complete? This may also involve a change to your site. You may go from a strictly informational site (before the invention is available for purchase) to an online retailer once the product is manufactured.

You may have a hard time answering the questions above, but it is good to address these issues. Spend time thinking through the answers instead of rushing through the creation of your site. You may discover you need help with any one of the above areas.

There are templates available online that can help you create your site if you want to do it yourself. Some sites offer free services, and others require a fee. For instance, **www.wordpress.com** is free, but **www.inowweb.com** charges.

ORGANIZING THE SITE

When you have figured out what you want to include on your site, it is time to decide how it should be organized. If your site is not well-organized, your customers will leave. There will be many sites with similar products to yours, and if your site is not user friendly, they will find one that is.

All sites have a home page — this is the landing page or the first page you see of the site. This is your chance to make a first impression. Therefore, your home page is important. The home page should convey immediately that the site is professional. It should include your company logo. The home pages on some sites change daily with daily updates to articles that appear on the home page. Other sites – more static sites—have a home page that will remain the same from day to day. If you decide that you want fresh content on your site each day, it must be updated on a daily basis. Use buttons, tabs, or drop-down menus to lead users to other parts of your site from your home page. You may want to include images on your home page. Again, look at other websites and take notes about what you like on other sites.

Other pages you may need include product descriptions, an "About Us" page, a shopping cart, and a contact page. Decide what information about yourself, your company, your process, and your background you want to be available on your site.

When you launch your site, you will need to promote it. The first thing you want to do is register your site with all of the search engines. Remember, simply registering with the search engines is not enough to get people to your site. You want people to be about to find your site and if your site is at the bottom of a search results list, people will not find you. The Internet is full of sites trying to get to the top of the results list in a search. You can pay a large amount of money to get your site to appear in the beginning of the results of a user search on a search engine, but there are other ways to drive traffic to your site — the ultimate goal. Remember, search engines determine which sites are at the top of the list based on relevance and the content of updates. Keep your info updated to ensure a spot at the top.

Be sure to let people know about your website. You can send out press releases announcing the launch as well as inform your acquaintances personally.

GETTING PEOPLE TO YOUR SITE

Even after all this research, planning, and designing, your website means nothing without visitors. You need people to be led to your site. With the millions of sites available on the Web, how do you get a user to your particular site? Back to the example of the baby bottle: If you search "baby bottle" on Google, you get 6,960,000 matches. You can have the most intricately designed website with a great layout, but it will do little good if no one visits the site.

There are a number of ways you can get people to your site. The most obvious is promoting your site through advertising, business cards, and word-of-mouth. You can also employ some techniques that will help your site move to the top of the results on a search engine.

Content

The content on your site is an opportunity for search engines to find your site, which will get you moved up in the rankings. If you are number 59,000,000 out of 59,600,000, you are going to have much fewer visitors than the number one site or a site on the first page of the results list.

By adding content, you are driving users to your site. According to marketing speaker David Meerman Scott, "…the single best thing you can do to improve your search engine marketing is to focus on building great content for your buyers."

In addition, good content on your site — content that people want to share with others — gives you the opportunity to be linked to other websites, such as social networking sites (which will be discussed later in this chapter). People on social networking sites, such as Facebook or Twitter, can post links to articles on other sites on their profiles. The more good content you have on your site, the more opportunity you have for users to promote the content for you.

Various types of content can make up your site, and the types you use will depend on your particular product and audience. Here are some types of content to consider for your website:

> **News stories:** News stories are timely and provide readers with the most up-to-date information about what is happening in the industry. They are objective pieces of content written in the third person.

> **Feature articles:** These are often longer than straight news stories but still fewer than 1,200 words.

> **Editorials:** These are opinion articles (like you find on the Op-Ed page of a newspaper). Experts in a given field generally write them, as those people are more credible and people care more about their opinions.

> **Images:** This includes photos and videos related to your video.

> **Announcements:** Use your website to post announcements about your company/invention. For example, if your product is featured on a new show or mentioned in an article in the New York *Times,* post an announcement and direct visitors to the story. Be sure to keep visitors of your site informed about the happenings in your company.

> **Interviews:** If you conduct an interview with an expert in your industry, you can post the Q&A on your website.

> **Interactive feature:** This includes surveys/polls, user feedback, discussion groups, forums, and chat.

SEO writing

By using keywords in the content of your website, search engine "crawlers" will locate your content and rank your site based on those keywords thereby increasing your rank on search pages. Using keywords to optimize your search results is known as **search engine optimization**.

As was mentioned earlier, companies can pay a large amount of money to appear in the first couple of pages of the search results. However, when the content on your site is loaded with keyword and keyword phrases, the search engine crawlers will find your site more easily, and you will move up in the results of search pages. The higher you are in search results, the more traffic your site gets. More traffic translates into more customers.

It is important to remember keywords will only bring potential customers to your site. Using a tool like Google Trends™ will show you what words or topics are popular at the moment. The content on the site must be dynamic and meet the needs of your audience in order for people to stay there and even recommend it to friends.

Needs

Your content must fit the needs of your audience. Think about why you search for things on the Internet. Your keywords will drive people to the site by moving the site up in rankings, but you must provide the content to keep them there and to bring them back the next time. Think about how you can fulfill the needs of your visitors with information on your site.

You want to also show consumers the benefits of your product(s) and your company. You want to stand out against competitors.

Updating your site

Once you get customers to your site, the goal is to keep them coming back. You want fresh content added to your site every day, or as often as possible. Much of your content will not change daily — such as your "about us" section — but by creating a space for "in the news" or "product updates," you give yourself something to periodically add to. A company blog is also a good idea. If your content stays the same every day, nothing drives a consumer to your site because the consumer will have read all of the information already. When you consistently update your site, the consumer has a reason to check back for updates and additional information.

Credibility

Be sure you represent yourself as a credible source. You never want to give out false information. You need to establish yourself as an honest organization. If you use sources for your content, be sure they are credible sources.

Other Tools

Besides the above mentioned, which should be definitely included, there are other options you can explore to market your product.

Blogging

Blogging is a great way to connect with an audience of customers and potential customers. A **blog** — short for Weblog — is published online, which makes it similar to a website. However, a blog is easier to update and can automatically notify other websites when you have added something new.

Derek Gehl, CEO of Internet Marketing Center, says a successful blog can "drive swarms of traffic to your main website, generate more product sales, create an additional stream of advertising income, be a great customer service tool, and much more."

Blogs are more informal and conversational than websites. Because of this, Gehl says, a blog "humanizes" your business — that is, showing there are human beings behind your business. In addition, a blog adds additional content to your website, which adds more opportunity for keywords to improve your site ranking.

A blog must be updated regularly to be successful. You need to provide your readers with fresh content every day. In addition, the writing should be useful but also interesting. It should provide readers with expertise and guidance.

Social networking

Social networking sites offer you yet another type of opportunity to market your invention and your business. These sites, such as Twitter, Facebook, MySpace, and LinkedIn, offer potential connections to millions and millions of people. People join these sites and link with their friends, co-workers, and acquaintances. These sites do provide an opportunity for you to get your name — or the name of your invention — out there. However, David Meerman Scott warns, "Marketing on these sites can be tricky because the online community on social networking sites hates overt commercial messages."

To use these social networking sites, you will first need to create a profile or page. For example on Facebook, when you visit the site you have the option of signing up for a personal or business profile; a product profile or a band profile. For the Burpee Baby Bottle, we could create a page for the product, a page for the business, or both. You fill in some personal information, agree to the terms and you have a page. You can then connect with people when they decide they like your product or business.

Scott says, "Every marketing and PR person should be aware of Twitter and understand how people use it." **Twitter** is a social networking site where users create "tweets," which Scott likens to away messages on instant messaging or status updates on Facebook. Users have 140 characters to update their "followers" about themselves or their business. For example, someone with a personal Twitter account might tweet about what they are doing during the day or something they want all of their followers to read. Businesses use Twitter for updates about upcoming specials/promotions or news in the industry. You have to be careful, warns Scott, that you do not use Twitter — or any social networking site — as an advertising outlet because it is free. You can mention deals that may relate to your company, but you cannot write, "Buy one, get one free!" as a tweet for your own company. However, you can say, "The next five people on the site get free tickets to a concert!" It is a fine line that should not be crossed.

How to Use E-mail and Newsgroups to Get Your Product in Front of Customers

As you attempt to get your new product or service in front of its target market and potential customers, you often become anxious to promote it and may be willing to go to great lengths to draw attention to it. Depending on which approach you take, you could gain attention that will make your product successful, or you could work just as hard and attract little or no attention to your product or service.

For example, e-mail is a common method of communication in today's technological world. Often, when people receive an e-mail they did not solicit, they simply delete it, discard any content it contained, and dismiss it as spam. As a businessperson, make sure that if you are going to send out mass e-mails, they at least gain some positive attention. Generally, they will be taken seriously only if the person receiving them solicited the information.

E-mail marketing is cost-effective and makes it easy to keep up consistent correspondence, which often leads to overuse by people anxious to get their products or services to the largest audience possible. Use e-mail marketing only to follow up with your customers or potential customers, or else e-mail will no longer be an effective tool. You want your customers to be the ones initiating the contact. This way, you know you are not wasting your time and effort creating e-mails and newsletters that will be simply deleted. It is also annoying for people to have their inboxes bombarded. This will allow you to send more informative, quality messages and newsletters because you know the recipients are interested in what you are saying or offering; you are not just sending it out to grab the attention of possible customers.

Places to find these potential customers include: other websites, e-mailing lists, and newsgroups, which are probably the most successful place for finding prospective customers for your product or service online. Be leery of e-mailing lists, especially if you are buying the lists from an outside source, because they could be fraudulent or lists of people who are sick of receiving too many e-mails;

A **newsgroup** is essentially a place online, called a "forum," where people who share the same interest can meet to share ideas. Use a search engine and find forums discussing topics that relate to your site, product, or service. Once you find these groups, monitor them and join the discussion. Establish yourself within the newsgroup. Be ready and available to answer questions and provide information requested in the newsgroup about the type of product or service you have. This will help develop your reputation as an industry expert, and it will keep your name and company name in the minds of these potential customers, who are obviously in your target market. If you handle these newsgroups correctly from the start, these forums can be one of the most powerful, cost-effective tools you have available to make new contacts and draw new visitors to your site. Be careful not to come across as pushy or someone only interested in making a sales pitch. The key is to develop a rapport with the participants of the newsgroup, establish your own credibility, and then give information on your product, service, or site. Present yourself in a way that will allow you to draw people to your site to obtain more information on what you have to offer.

Once you are well established and have received inquiries on your product or service, use a major Internet browser, such as Internet Explorer or Mozilla, to download your newsletter or post messages to the newsgroup of your choice. Again, make sure you are posting informative articles and messages directly relating to your specific company, product, or service. Be sure your newsletter or post does not come across as a sales letter or sales pitch, or at least not an obvious one. Create these newsletters to give out just enough information to draw those potential customers and current customers to your site for more. Once you get them to your site, you can ask them to subscribe to your e-mail newsletter.

If used correctly, these newsgroups can even be the foundation for creating an e-mail list because addresses obtained in this method would be from participants who have inquired about your company, product, or service. These potential customers will want to stay updated on information and promotions about your product.

E-mail marketing and newsgroups can be two of the cheapest, most successful ways to market your product and get it in front of potential customers, but you have to take the time to make sure you do it correctly, or it could just as easily be of no help. You have worked so hard to create and develop your product, and it is finally ready to put in front of customers. Take some time to research these cheap and often highly successful resources to promote your invention and make potential buyers aware of your company.

CHAPTER 13:

Beware of Scam Artists

"Anyone who wants to sell you
overnight success or wealth is not
interested in your success; they
are interested in your money."

— BO BENNETT, AUTHOR AND BUSINESSMAN

If It Sounds Too Good to Be True...

Commercializing your invention is a complicated process. It requires diverse skills and expertise that few inventors possess. Most need some professional advice and assistance at some point in the process. Why not hire an invention marketing firm and hand the headache over to them?

Many firms advertise invention marketing services on television, the Internet, and in magazines. They claim they will get your product onto store shelves. They lure in inventors with a small fee for an initial assessment of your invention's potential. They deliver the good news that your invention will make you millions, and then they ask for $10,000 to take your invention marketing through the next steps. To an inexperienced inventor, this may mean relief from the business aspect of inventing. The fee may seem to be worth the price for the amount of services being offered. The firm has essentially told you, you will make millions, so why not invest with them?

Be careful. According to the American Society of Inventors (**www.asoi.org**), invention marketing scams cost inventors $300 million a year. In April 2006, a federal judge ordered the invention marketing firm Davison and Associates to pay back $26 million to inventors ripped off by what the court called their "blatant, varied, and repeated misrepresentations." These misrepresentations included false claims about how selective they are regarding which inventions to promote, the objectivity of their market analyses, the percentage of clients whose inventions became profitable, their partnerships with manufacturers, and the source of their income. The firm claimed their income came from sharing royalties with successful clients, when actually their profits came from the exorbitant fees (up to $12,000) they charged inventors for performing almost no meaningful work.

This case may seem outrageous, but it is a warning to do homework about potential invention marketing firms.

The hook: Free invention evaluations or assessments

If a firm advertises itself as an invention promotion or marketing firm and is not part of a university, government agency, or a nonprofit, it is highly likely to be a scam. There are professionals who can help inventors at various stages of the commercialization process, but few legitimate invention marketing or promotion firms take products from the concept stage to manufacturing or licensing. If a firm claims to do it all, beware, and check the resources listed in this chapter to see if other inventors think the company has ripped them off.

Invention marketing scammers perpetrate a variety of scam angles. The most prevalent are:

➤ Providing an invention evaluation report that encourages you to pursue commercialization of a product regardless of its actual merit. The company can then charge further fees for additional, worthless services.

➤ Claiming to make money off of royalties when all income is made from fees charged to inventors.

➤ Conducting incomplete patent searches and not rendering any legal opinion about patentability.

➤ Charging large fees to submit a simple and inexpensive provisional patent application, and representing it as a regular patent application.

➤ Selling marketing services based on nonexistent connections with manufacturers and other prospective licensees, and charging high fees to deliver standard lists of manufacturers anyone can obtain for him or herself.

The first service an invention promotion firm will offer you is an "objective" assessment of your invention's potential. Someone who wants you to pay large fees for pretend work on your invention will tell you your invention is worth pursuing; inventors' natural enthusiasm for their inventions makes them gullible.

Scam artists will take advantage of your enthusiasm and skewed perspective. This "objective" assessment is more often than not free. This is the bait that scam artists use to hook inventors.

Pricier services

Once you are hooked with the firm's glowing response to your invention, the company will ask you to pay a moderate amount, less than $1,000, for its services. What the promoter may not tell you is this money pays for the next service, but you will not get much for your money. You will get just enough to string you along and get you to purchase the subsequent, even higher-cost service the promoter will try to sell you next. The company may try to sell you a marketing report, business plan, list of manufacturers, patent search, patent application, or a professional sketch or other type of artwork that shows your invention. By paying upfront fees for a package of services of unknown value, you open yourself up to receiving worthless services.

Scammers often sell inventors off-the-shelf marketing reports and business plans that have little relevance to the invention and industry in which the inventor is working. These products have no value, but they move the scam along. The reason inventors keep sinking money into scams is they feel that because they have paid so much already, they had better keep going to get something out of it. This mentality, combined with the gullibility of idealists who really believe in their product, makes inventors prime pickings for scammers.

Lists of manufacturers

Scammers often say they have contacts at manufacturing firms or even that they represent firms looking for inventors. What they deliver to inventors is usually a list of Standard Industrial Classification (SIC) or North

American Industry Classification System (NAICS) codes. According to the U.S. Census Bureau, NAICS is "the standard used by Federal statistical agencies in classifying business establishments for the purpose of collecting, analyzing, and publishing statistical data related to the U.S. business economy."

Patent searches and applications

Invention promotion firms often offer patent searches. Because your patent application can be rejected if your invention has been publicly disclosed by anyone at any time, an extremely broad and thorough search is required. The USPTO searches many sources to verify the uniqueness of your claim, including:

> Its own database of existing U.S. patents

> Foreign patents

> Any published document

> Technical books and manuals

> Doctoral dissertations

> Scientific articles and research reports in journals and magazines

> Industry and corporate brochures and reports from fields related to your invention

There are legitimate firms that conduct thorough patent searches. No one can guarantee he or she can find every source a USPTO examiner will use or guarantee your patent will be granted. Avoid any firm that does offer such a guarantee. To increase your odds of obtaining a thorough patent search, work with a patent agent, many of whom are former USPTO examiners. Others are professionals working for legitimate firms located in the Washington, D.C., area. They have access to the USPTO's physical files. All patent agents must be certified to practice in front of the USPTO.

Scammers may offer to help you obtain a patent. Instead of a regular patent, however, you likely will receive low-value services for high prices. You might find yourself with a provisional patent you could have filed yourself for a small fee. It is best to use patent attorneys or agents for this instead.

Having just a provisional patent is dangerous because it starts a 12-month clock ticking within which time you must file a regular patent application or your invention will be deemed publicly disclosed and unpatentable. Provisional patents can be great tools for inventors at the right stage in the process, but paying too much to obtain one at the wrong time can be disastrous. Paying a big fee for a **boilerplate**, or a standard document formulation, marketing report or overpaying for artwork may or may not bankrupt you, but it will set you back the thousands of dollars in patent application, examination, and research fees only to find yourself unable to patent your invention.

The trouble is it is exceedingly difficult to tell the good guys from the bad guys, and most inventors will need professional advice along the way. Some invention promotion scam firms even hire manufacturers to act as either phony references or to license and manufacture money-losing inventions and pay a few select customers royalties so those customers will unwittingly offer praise for the company.

Attorney generals from many states have successfully prosecuted invention marketing scammers. This is little comfort to individuals whose savings have been stolen and whose ideas are no longer patentable because they were disclosed and not protected.

What Legitimate Services Look Like

Although many invention evaluation organizations charge a few hundred dollars for an evaluation, legitimate agents or representatives who market inventions to prospective licensees charge royalties only. *See the list of university, government, and nonprofit invention evaluation organizations in Chapter 3.* These two activities are separate functions. Legitimate invention evaluators will charge a fee to offset their overhead costs. Scammers will offer a free assessment. Legitimate marketers such as agents and representatives will charge a royalty, or some percentage of your sales, to represent your product, while scammers will charge a flat fee to provide you off-the-shelf marketing reports and impersonalized, publicly available lists of contacts at manufacturing firms.

You can get real information concerning inventing processes, pitfalls, and techniques from a variety of legitimate sources. One is inventor clubs or associations. The website for the PBS show *Everyday Edisons* has a list of inventor associations in various American cities at **www.everydayedisons. com** under the Resources section. *Inventors Digest* magazine and the United Inventors Association (**www.uiausa.com**) are both well-regarded independent inventor resources. Polson Enterprises, a firm that provides engineering services to boat-part builders and inventors, has a useful and informative website with tips on a variety of invention-related products at **www.virtualpet.com/invention**.

How to Avoid Being Scammed

Before purchasing any invention evaluation or marketing services, check out the firm you are considering working with on one of the following websites and call your state attorney general's office (often they have toll-free numbers) or the Better Business Bureau to see whether the firm has complaints against it.

Websites dedicated to unmasking inventor scammers include:

> Inventor Ed's Invention Promoter and Caution Lists at **www.inventored.org/caution/list**. This site has lists of companies known to have problems or complaints. The companies are broken into three lists: the "Watch List," the "Extreme Caution" list, and the "ISC List," which lists alias names and associates of the Invention Submission Corp.

> The complaint site on the USPTO site is at **www.uspto.gov/web/offices/com/iip/complaints.htm**. Here, the USPTO publishes the complaints it receives about potential scams.

Protect yourself

The best way to protect yourself before working with any firm is to do the following things:

> Avoid firms that advertise on TV, radio, and in magazines and ask you to call a toll-free number.

> Ask for the total cost of the firm's services.

> Work with firms that specialize in one stage of the invention promotion process (for example, patent searching, patent applications, or market research).

> Ask for and check the firm's references, including clients. If the firm claims to have a network of manufacturers waiting to license inventors' products, check with those manufacturers by calling and

investigating. The list should be long, but you can randomly select a few clients and firms to call.

➢ Check the name of any firm you are considering working with against the list provided on Inventor Ed's site and the complaints list on the USPTO site.

➢ Talk to fellow inventors. *See the Appendix for a state-by-state list of inventor clubs and a list of national inventor associations.*

➢ Read the contract before you sign it, and be sure it lists all the services the firm said it would provide.

➢ Ask for any guarantees in writing, and ask whether the firm will provide written results of its patent and invention assessment work.

Ask key questions

Per the American Inventors Protection Act of 1999, invention marketing firms must disclose:

➢ How many inventions they have evaluated during the past five years.

➢ How many of these received positive evaluations and how many received negative.

➢ How many clients contracted with them during the past five years.

➢ How many clients made net financial profits as a result of their services.

➢ How many clients received licensing agreements.

➢ All of the invention promotion companies they have been affiliated with over the past ten years. This includes the names of the companies as well as their addresses.

Most legitimate firms provide unqualified positive assessments to about 5 percent or less of the inventors who contact them. Legitimate firms work with a few select ideas and have a decent but not suspiciously high rate of success. Because they take on only about 5 percent of inventors who contact them, they do a good job of helping the ones they pick. Remember, many firms lie about these figures, have been successfully prosecuted, and have paid large fines. Many of these firms are still in business. This is a testament to how much money these scam artists make off of gullible inventors. Remain skeptical and insist on answers in writing.

You also want to find out if a company has ever been investigated by the Federal Trade Commission or any state attorney general's office. This can help you decide whether this is a firm you want to work with. Ask what industry the firm specializes in. If it claims to help inventors with everything from food products to medical devices, toys, and sports equipment, be skeptical. Not only is the process of commercializing an invention made up of discrete steps that higher-quality firms specialize in, but invention promoters who claim to have contacts with potential licensees also must specialize by industry. There is no realistic way these firms could effectively keep up with multiple markets. (Note that consumer items such as home and gift products can be lumped into a single category.)

Be skeptical of any firm that provides only encouraging and unqualified feedback about your invention's likely success. Most invention ideas start out with significant shortcomings, many of which may be addressed as you learn more about the field. If it sounds too good to be true, it probably is. Find out how the firm really makes its money. If it offers a free evaluation then requests a lump sum upfront from inventors, it is most likely a scam. If it makes most of its money from royalties, ask for documentation on this and ask why the company charges fees for marketing reports and other services.

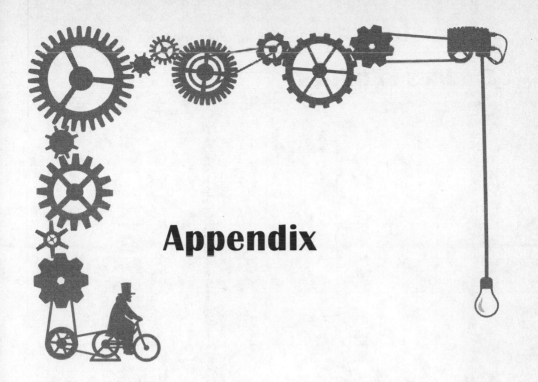

Appendix

Business Entities

Legal entity	Costs involved	Number of owners	Paperwork	Tax implications	Liability issues
Sole Proprietorship	Local fees assessed for registering business; generally between $25 and $100	One	Local licenses and registrations; assumed name registration	Owner is responsible for all personal and business taxes	Owner is personally liable for all financial and legal transactions
Partnership	Local fees assessed for registering business; generally between $25 and $100	Two or more	Partnership agreement	Business income passes through to partners and is taxed at the individual level only	Partners are personally liable for all financial and legal transactions, including those of the other partners
LLC	Filing fees for articles of incorporation; generally between $100 and $800, depending on the state	One or more	Articles of organization; operating agreement	Business income passes through to owners and is taxed at the individual level only	Owners are protected from liability; company carries all liability regarding financial and legal transactions
Corporation	Varies with each state, can range from $100 to $500	One or more; must designate directors and officers	Articles of incorporation to be filed with state; quarterly and annual report requirements; annual meeting reports	Corporation is taxed as a legal entity; income earned from business is taxed at individual level	Owners are protected from liability; company carries all liability regarding financial and legal transactions

Personal Skills Inventory

Verbal skills

- Performing in front of groups
- Entertaining in front of groups
- Public speaking
- Interviewing people
- Selling ideas, products, or services
- Debating

Written skills

- Writing technical language, reports, and/or manuals
- Writing poetry
- Writing fiction
- Writing screenplays
- Preparing and writing reports
- Writing sales and advertising copy
- Editing and proofreading written material
- Writing case studies
- Writing treatment plans
- Writing press releases
- Typing

Training/Consulting

- Teaching
- Advising
- Coaching
- Presenting
- Facilitating a group
- Developing curriculum
- Consulting
- Recommending solutions

Research

- Searching written sources for information
- Searching technological sources for information
- Interviewing sources
- Compiling data
- Documenting research results

Management

- Managing personnel
- Managing projects
- Delegating responsibilities
- Training staff
- Facilitating conflict management

Financial

- Calculating numbers
- Maintaining accurate financial records
- Creating computer-generated charts and/or graphs
- Creating budgets
- Balancing budgets

Creative

- Creating visual images (i.e., photography, video production, or website design)
- Painting
- Sculpting
- Drawing
- Writing music
- Performing music
- Acting

Sample Consumer Questionnaire

1.	Have you ever purchased any _____ products? (List product category.)

2.	What types of _____ products have you purchased in the past 12 months?

3.	Why did you purchase these products?

4.	About how much did you pay for these products?

5.	Would you use a product that _____? (Describe benefits of your product.)

6.	Would you buy such a product?

7.	How much would you expect to pay for a product like that?

8.	What would be the most important features, functions, purposes, or benefits of such a product?

Sample Confidentiality or
Nondisclosure Agreement

It is understood and agreed to that the below identified discloser of confidential information may provide certain information that is and must be kept confidential. To ensure the protection of such information, and to preserve any confidentiality necessary under patent and/or trade secret laws, it is agreed that

1. The Confidential Information to be disclosed can be described as and includes:

Invention description(s), technical and business information relating to proprietary ideas and inventions, ideas, patentable ideas, trade secrets, drawings and/or illustrations, patent searches, existing and/or contemplated products and services, research and development, production, costs, profit and margin information, finances and financial projections, customers, clients, marketing, and current or future business plans and models, regardless of whether such information is designated as "Confidential Information" at the time of its disclosure.

2. The Recipient agrees not to disclose the confidential information obtained from the discloser to anyone unless required to do so by law.

3. This Agreement states the entire agreement between the parties concerning the disclosure of Confidential Information. Any addition or modification to this Agreement must be made in writing and signed by the parties.

4. If any of the provisions of this Agreement are found to be unenforceable, the remainder shall be enforced as fully as possible and the unenforceable provision(s) shall be deemed modified to the limited extent required to permit enforcement of the Agreement as a whole.

WHEREFORE, the parties acknowledge that they have read and understand this Agreement and voluntarily accept the duties and obligations set forth herein.

Recipient of Confidential Information:

Name (Print or Type): _____

Signature: _____   Date: _____

Discloser of Confidential Information:

Name (Print or Type): _____

Signature: _____
Signature: _____
Date: _____

SOURCE: **WWW.IPWATCHDOG.COM/TRADESECRET/SIMPLE-CONFIDENTIALITY-AGREEMENT**

Intellectual Property Protections and Their Features

Types of Patents

Patent rights establish your priority if others apply for a patent on the same idea. If someone else applies for a patent, this documentation can establish the date by which you invented the item to give your claim priority over a competing claim.

Functional features are elements of your invention that relate to how it works. Nonfunctional features are design, aesthetic, decorative, and packaging elements of your invention.

Provisional	Utility	Design	Plant
What it protects			
Patent rights	The functional features of a process, item, machine, or improvement on an existing invention	The nonfunctional features of a process, item, or machine	Plants reproduced asexually or through grafts or cuttings
What is required			
A description of the invention; provisional patent application	Proof that the invention is useful, novel, and nonobvious based on specific descriptive claims; utility patent application	Design patent application	Plant patent application
Cost*			
Application filing fee: $110	Application filing fee: $165; $82 for electronic filing	Application filing fee: $110	Application filing fee: $110

Provisional	Utility	Design	Plant
Method of protection			
Establishes a filing date with the USPTO so you can file a patent application up to a year later and use the provisional patent date as the patent filing date	Permits the patent holder to sue individuals or organizations that infringe on the patent's specific claims and recover royalties and possibly damages		
Method of enforcement			
You must apply for a patent and then pursue infringers.	Civil court		
Time from application to protection			
Immediate	Protection begins when the patent is issued, frequently 18 months to three years after application.	Protection begins when patent is issued.	
Length of protection			
One year	20 years from date of application (at least 17 years; if examination takes more than three years, you can request an extension)	14 years from date of application	20 years from date of application

Provisional	Utility	Design	Plant
Notes, caveats, and drawbacks			
If you publicly disclose your idea then fail to pursue a patent within one year, you will lose the right to patent the invention, as it will be public knowledge. Also covers only features described in the application. If significant features are not described or are added or changed, you must submit a new provisional application. You must apply for foreign patent rights within one year of the provisional application.	Expensive and complicated to pursue; application gets published, revealing details of your invention even if a patent is not issued; if done poorly, the patent claims can be circumvented by competitors who engineer around them	Only applies to nonfunctional features	Only for use with plants

* MAINTENANCE FEES ARE PAID AT 3.5, 7.5, AND 11.5 YEARS AFTER THE PATENT IS ISSUED.

* COST: USPTO FEES CAN CHANGE. THESE ARE THE MINIMUM FEES. THEY REFLECT FEES FOR INDIVIDUALS AND SMALL ORGANIZATIONS AND DO NOT INCLUDE FEES FOR AMENDMENTS, LATE FEES, SURCHARGES FOR EXCESSIVE NUMBER OF CLAIMS, AND APPEALS, JUST TO NAME A FEW.

THE COSTS LISTED ARE SIMPLY THE COSTS OF APPLICATION OR REGISTRATION; THEY DO NOT REFLECT ANY COSTS OF HIRING EXPERTS TO RESEARCH, WRITE, OR REVIEW YOUR APPLICATIONS.

Other Formal Intellectual Property Protections

	Trademarks	Copyright
What it protects	Product name or logo	Original written works, artwork, music, and computer software
What is required	A word or symbol that represents or brands an invention, item, product, or service (in the case of the service mark) and distinguishes it from other similar products or services	A work need only be made public to be considered copyrighted. Registration with the USPTO can provide a basis for monetary damages.
Cost*	Once the mark is in use, it is a right granted by common law (automatically) for free. Better protection can be gained through registration with the USPTO, filing fee $325 (electronic) or $375 (paper); state fees vary; trade association applications may be free with association membership.	Once the work is published or performed publicly, the copyright is granted by common law (automatically) for free. Better protection can be gained through registration with the Library of Congress, application fee $45.
Method of protection	Permits owner to sue individuals or organizations that use the same name or logo, even for different types of products	Permits owner to sue individuals or organizations that use or copy the work without the owner's permission
Method of enforcement	Civil court	Civil court
Time from application to protection	Immediate upon use of mark in commerce	Immediate upon publication
Length of protection	Forever, unless the mark becomes generic through use as a product description rather than a name	70 years after creator's death or 120 years for work for hire
Notes, caveats, and drawbacks	Trademarks work well in concert with patents. Patent protection is time-limited, but once a patent expires, the association of the invention with a strong trademark or brand name can help maintain market share against competitors indefinitely.	

* COST: USPTO FEES CAN CHANGE. THESE ARE THE MINIMUM FEES.

Informal Intellectual Property Protections

	Detailed records and witness signatures	Trade secrets
What it protects	Patent rights	Functional features
What is required	Inventor-signed and dated documentation of each step of the inventor's thought process. Also helpful are signed and dated statements by credible witnesses.	Secrecy
Cost	Free	Free
Method of protection	Establishes date of invention by inventor in the eyes of the USPTO in the event of competing patent claims	Nondisclosure agreements. Secret holders can sue individuals who steal their secrets or pay others to do so.
Method of enforcement	Inventor must apply for a patent then pursue infringers.	Civil court
Length of protection	Until a patent is granted to this inventor or another inventor	Forever
Notes, caveats and drawbacks	Not a registration with an official agency, simply a means of establishing priority (meaning you thought of it first)	Must be kept secret; rights cease if secret is disclosed to anyone, even a person other than one who copies the secret; can be circumvented through reverse engineering; cannot protect against another inventor developing the same process or product on their own, even if done systematically and purposely to defeat your protection.

Patent Fee Schedule

Type of Fee	Fee for Small Entities	Regular Fee
Utility Basic Filing Fee	$165	$330
Utility Basic Filing Fee – Electronic Fee for Small Entities	$82	N/A
Design Basic Filing Fee	$110	$220
Plant Basic Filing Fee	$110	$220
Reissue Basic Filing Fee*	$165	$330
Application Size Fee (for each 50 pages over 100 pages in the patent application)	$135	$270
Utility Search Fee	$270	$540
Design Search Fee	$50	$100
Plant Search Fee	$165	$330
Reissue Search Fee	$270	$540
Utility Examination Fee	$110	$220
Design Examination Fee	$70	$140
Plant Examination Fee	$85	$170
Reissue Examination Fee	$325	$650
Utility Issue Fee	$755	$1,510
Design Issue Fee	$430	$860
Patent Issue Fee	$595	$1,190
Reissue Issue Fee	$755	$1,510
Publication fee for early, voluntary, or normal publication	$300	$300
Patent Maintenance Fees: 3.5 years	$490	$980
Patent Maintenance Fees: 7.5 years	$1,240	$2,480
Patent Maintenance Fees: 11.5 years	$2,055	$4,110
Patent Maintenance Fees Surcharge: 3.5 year - Late payment within 6 months	$65	$130
Patent Maintenance Fees Surcharge: 7.5 year - Late payment within 6 months	$65	$130
Patent Maintenance Fees Surcharge: 11.5 year - Late payment within 6 months	$65	$130

Patent Maintenance Fees: Surcharge after expiration - Late payment is unavoidable	$700	$700
Patent Maintenance Fees: Surcharge after expiration - Late payment is unintentional	$1,640	$1,640
Processing fee, except in provisional applications	$130	$130
Processing fee for provisional applications	$50	$50
Request for expedited examination of a design application	$900	$900
Non-English specification	$130	$130

*REISSUE IS "AN APPLICATION FOR A PATENT TO TAKE THE PLACE OF AN UNEXPIRED PATENT THAT IS DEFECTIVE IN ONE OR MORE PARTICULARS (ITEMS OR DETAILS)," ACCORDING TO THE USPTO.

SOURCE: **WWW.USPTO.GOV**, AS OF SEPTEMBER 2010

Trademark Fee Schedule

Type of Fee	Fee for Small Entities	Regular Fee
Application for Registration: Paper Filing	$375	$375
Application for Registration: Electronic Filing (Trademark Electronic Application System Application)	$325	$325
Application for Registration: Electronic Filing (Trademark Electronic Application System Plus Application)	$275	$275
Application for Renewal, per class	$400	$400
Additional fee for filing renewal application during the grace period, per class	$100	$100
Correcting a deficiency in a renewal application	$100	$100

SOURCE: **WWW.USPTO.GOV**, AS OF SEPTEMBER 2010

Utility Patent Application

PTO/SB/05 (08-08)
Approved for use through 06/30/2010. OMB 0651-0032
U.S. Patent and Trademark Office. U.S. DEPARTMENT OF COMMERCE
Under the Paperwork Reduction Act of 1995, no persons are required to respond to a collection of information unless it displays a valid OMB control number.

UTILITY PATENT APPLICATION TRANSMITTAL	
Attorney Docket No.	
First Inventor	
Title	
Express Mail Label No.	

(Only for new nonprovisional applications under 37 CFR 1.53(b))

APPLICATION ELEMENTS
See MPEP chapter 600 concerning utility patent application contents.

ADDRESS TO: Commissioner for Patents
P.O. Box 1450
Alexandria VA 22313-1450

1. ☐ Fee Transmittal Form (e.g., PTO/SB/17)
2. ☐ Applicant claims small entity status.
   See 37 CFR 1.27.
3. ☐ Specification [Total Pages_____]
   Both the claims and abstract must start on a new page
   (For information on the preferred arrangement, see MPEP 608.01(a))
4. ☐ Drawing(s) (35 U.S.C. 113) [Total Sheets _____]
5. Oath or Declaration [Total Sheets _____]
   a. ☐ Newly executed (original or copy)
   b. ☐ A copy from a prior application (37 CFR 1.63(d))
      (for continuation/divisional with Box 18 completed)
      i. ☐ DELETION OF INVENTOR(S)
         Signed statement attached deleting inventor(s)
         name in the prior application, see 37 CFR
         1.63(d)(2) and 1.33(b).
6. ☐ Application Data Sheet. See 37 CFR 1.76
7. ☐ CD-ROM or CD-R in duplicate, large table or
      Computer Program (Appendix)
      ☐ Landscape Table on CD
8. Nucleotide and/or Amino Acid Sequence Submission
   (If applicable, items a. – c. are required)
   a. ☐ Computer Readable Form (CRF)
   b. Specification Sequence Listing on:
      i. ☐ CD-ROM or CD-R (2 copies); or
      ii. ☐ Paper
   c. ☐ Statements verifying identity of above copies

ACCOMPANYING APPLICATION PARTS

9. ☐ Assignment Papers (cover sheet (PTO-1595) & document(s))
   Name of Assignee_____
   _____
10. ☐ 37 CFR 3.73(b) Statement   ☐ Power of Attorney
    (when there is an assignee)
11. ☐ English Translation Document (if applicable)
12. ☐ Information Disclosure Statement (PTO/SB/08 or PTO-1449)
    ☐ Copies of foreign patent documents,
       publications, & other information
13. ☐ Preliminary Amendment
14. ☐ Return Receipt Postcard (MPEP 503)
    (Should be specifically itemized)
15. ☐ Certified Copy of Priority Document(s)
    (if foreign priority is claimed)
16. ☐ Nonpublication Request under 35 U.S.C. 122(b)(2)(B)(i).
    Applicant must attach form PTO/SB/35 or equivalent.
17. ☐ Other:_____
    _____

18. If a CONTINUING APPLICATION, check appropriate box, and supply the requisite information below and in the first sentence of the specification following the title, or in an Application Data Sheet under 37 CFR 1.76:

☐ Continuation   ☐ Divisional   ☐ Continuation-in-part (CIP)   of prior application No.:_____

Prior application information: Examiner_____   Art Unit:_____

19. CORRESPONDENCE ADDRESS

☐ The address associated with Customer Number: [_____]   OR   ☐ Correspondence address below

Name	
Address	

City		State		Zip Code	
Country		Telephone		Email	

Signature		Date	
Name (Print/Type)		Registration No. (Attorney/Agent)	

This collection of information is required by 37 CFR 1.53(b). The information is required to obtain or retain a benefit by the public which is to file (and by the USPTO to process) an application. Confidentiality is governed by 35 U.S.C. 122 and 37 CFR 1.11 and 1.14. This collection is estimated to take 12 minutes to complete, including gathering, preparing, and submitting the completed application form to the USPTO. Time will vary depending upon the individual case. Any comments on the amount of time you require to complete this form and/or suggestions for reducing this burden, should be sent to the Chief Information Officer, U.S. Patent and Trademark Office, U.S. Department of Commerce, P.O. Box 1450, Alexandria, VA 22313-1450. DO NOT SEND FEES OR COMPLETED FORMS TO THIS ADDRESS. SEND TO: Commissioner for Patents, P.O. Box 1450, Alexandria, VA 22313-1450.

If you need assistance in completing the form, call 1-800-PTO-9199 and select option 2.

Copyright Application

· ·

 UNITED STATES COPYRIGHT OFFICE
Form CO · Application for Copyright Registration

| Print Form |
| Clear Form |

APPLICATION FOR COPYRIGHT REGISTRATION

* Designates Required Fields

1 WORK BEING REGISTERED

1a. * Type of work being registered (*Fill in one only*)

- ☐ Literary work
- ☐ Visual arts work
- ☐ Sound recording
- ☐ Performing arts work
- ☐ Motion picture/audiovisual work
- ☐ Single serial issue

ApplicationForCopyrightRegistration

1b. * Title of this work (*one title per space*) [Remove]

WorkTitles

[Click here to create space to add an additional title]

1c. For a serial issue: Volume [ ] Number [ ] Issue [ ] ISSN [ ]

Frequency of publication: [ ] Other [ ]

1d. Previous or alternative title

1e. * Year of completion [ ][ ][ ][ ]

Publication (*If this work has not been published, skip to section 2*)

1f. Date of publication [ ] (*mm/dd/yyyy*) **1g.** ISBN [ ]

1h. Nation of publication ☐ United States ☐ Other [Clear Response] Other [ ]

1i. Published as a contribution in a larger work entitled

1j. If line 1i above names a serial issue Volume [ ] Number [ ] Issue [ ]

On pages [ ]

1k. If work was preregistered Number PRE- [ ][ ][ ][ ][ ][ ][ ][ ][ ][ ][ ]

Page of

UNITED STATES COPYRIGHT OFFICE

Form CO · Application for Copyright Registration

Print Form

Clear Form

For Office Use Only

WorkBeingRegistered

2 AUTHOR INFORMATION - Entry Number

Remove Item

2a. Personal name   *complete either 2a or 2b*

First Name | Middle | Last

2b. Organization name

2c. Doing business as

2d. Year of birth   **2e.** Year of death

2f. * ☐ Citizenship   ☐ United States   ☐ Other   Other   Clear
          ☐ Domicile   ☐ United States   ☐ Other   Other   Clear

2g. Author's contribution: ☐ Made for hire   ☐ Anonymous
                                 ☐ Pseudonymous   (Pseudonym is:)

Continuation of Author Information

2h. * This author created *(Fill in only the authorship that applies to this author)*

☐ Text/poetry   ☐ Compilation   ☐ Map/technical drawing   ☐ Music
☐ Editing   ☐ Sculpture   ☐ Architectural work   ☐ Lyrics
☐ Computer program   ☐ Jewelry design   ☐ Photography   ☐ Motion picture/audiovisual
☐ Collective work   ☐ 2-dimensional artwork ☐ Script/play/screenplay ☐ Sound recording/performance

Other:

For Office Use Only

AuthorInformation

Page of

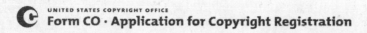

UNITED STATES COPYRIGHT OFFICE
Form CO · Application for Copyright Registration

Print Form

Clear Form

Click here to create space to add an additional author

3 COPYRIGHT CLAIMANT INFORMATION - Entry Number

Remove Item

Clear Section

Claimant *complete either 3a or 3b* - If you do not know the address for a claimant, enter "not known" in the Street address and City fields.

3a. Personal name

First Name

Middle

Last

3b. Organization name

3c. Doing business as

3d. Street address *

Street address (line 2)

City *

State

ZIP / Postal code

Country

Email

Phone number

(Add "+" and country code for foreign numbers)

3e. If claimant is **not** an author, copyright ownership acquired by: ☐ Written agreement ☐ Will or inheritance ☐ Other   Clear

Other

For Office Use Only

CopyrightClaimantInformation

Click here to create space to add an additional claimant

4 LIMITATION OF COPYRIGHT CLAIM

Skip section 4 if this work is all new.

4a. Material excluded from this claim *(Material previously registered, previously published, or not owned by this claimant)*

☐ Text ☐ Artwork ☐ Music ☐ Sound recording/performance ☐ Motion picture/audiovisual

Other:

Page of

Print Form

Clear Form

UNITED STATES COPYRIGHT OFFICE

Form CO · Application for Copyright Registration

4b. Previous registration(s)   Number [ ]   Year [ ][ ][ ][ ]

Number [ ]   Year [ ][ ][ ][ ]

4c. New material included in this claim (*This work contains new, additional, or revised material*)

- [ ] Text
- [ ] Compilation
- [ ] Map/technical drawing
- [ ] Music
- [ ] Poetry
- [ ] Sculpture
- [ ] Architectural work
- [ ] Lyrics
- [ ] Computer program
- [ ] Jewelry design
- [ ] Photography
- [ ] Motion picture/audiovisual
- [ ] Editing
- [ ] 2-dimensional artwork
- [ ] Script/play/screenplay
- [ ] Sound recording/performance

Other: [ ]

For Office Use Only

LimitationOfCopyrightClaim

5 RIGHTS AND PERMISSIONS CONTACT

Clear Section

- [ ] Check if information below should be copied from the **first** copyright claimant

First Name [ ]   Middle [ ]   Last [ ]

Name of organization [ ]

Street address [ ]

Street address (line 2) [ ]

City [ ]   State [ ]   ZIP / Postal code [ ]   Country [ ]

Email [ ]   Phone number [ ]   (*Add "+" and country code for foreign numbers*)

Page of

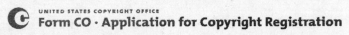

UNITED STATES COPYRIGHT OFFICE

Form CO · Application for Copyright Registration

| Print Form |
| Clear Form |

For Office Use Only

RightsAndPermissionsContact

6 CORRESPONDENCE CONTACT

☐ Copy from **first** copyright claimant   ☐ Copy from rights and permissions contact

First name *   Middle   Last *

Name of organization

Street address *

Street address (line 2)

City *   State   ZIP / Postal code   Country

Email *   Daytime phone number   *(Add "+" and country code for foreign numbers)*

For Office Use Only

CorrespondenceContact

7 MAIL CERTIFICATE TO:

* Complete either 7a, 7b, or both

☐ Copy from **first** copyright claimant   ☐ Copy from rights and permissions contact   ☐ Copy from correspondence contact

7a. First Name   Middle   Last

Page of

UNITED STATES COPYRIGHT OFFICE

Form CO · Application for Copyright Registration

Print Form

Clear Form

7b. Name of organization

7c. Street address *

Street address (line 2)

City *	State	ZIP / Postal code	Country

For Office Use Only

MailCertificateTo

8 CERTIFICATION

17 U.S.C. § 506(e): Any person who knowingly makes a false representation of a material fact in the application for copyright registration provided for by section 409, or in any written statement filed in connection with the application, shall be fined not more than $2,500.

I certify that I am the author, copyright claimant, or owner of exclusive rights, or the authorized agent of the author, copyright claimant, or owner of exclusive rights, of this work, and that the information given in this application is correct to the best of my knowledge.

8a. Handwritten signature

8b. Printed name

⦿ Today's date   ◯ Write date by hand

8c. Date signed

8d. Deposit account number   Account holder

8e. Applicant's internal tracking number (optional)

Page of

UNITED STATES COPYRIGHT OFFICE
Form CO · Instructions

Use this form to register a

- *Literary work*
- *Visual arts work*
- *Performing arts work*
- *Motion picture or other audiovisual work*
- *Sound recording*
- *Single serial issue*

Before you register your work

Review the appropriate circulars on the Copyright Office website, www.copyright.gov, for detailed information about how to register particular types of works and the requirements for what copy or copies of your work to send. Also, consider using the electronic Copyright Office (eCO) for faster service and a lower filing fee.

What may be included

The following may be included in one registration on Form CO:

- ***Unpublished works:*** *works by the same author(s) and owned by the same copyright claimant(s), organized in a collection under a collection title.*
- ***Published works:*** *works published in a single unit of publication and owned by the same copyright claimant.*

What to send

1 Completed and signed application

2 $50 filing fee payable to *Register of Copyrights*

3 Deposit—the required copy or copies of your work
   - *Unpublished works:* one complete copy.
   - *Published works:* generally, two complete copies of the "best edition." There are exceptions for certain types of works. See Circular 1, *Copyright Basics*, for details.

To avoid damage to your deposit from Library security measures, please package the following items in boxes rather than envelopes for mailing to the Copyright Office:
- electronic media such as audiocassettes, videocassettes, CDs, and DVDs
- microform
- photographs
- slick advertisements and color photocopies

Also please note that CDs packaged in standard full-sized jewel boxes are more likely to survive the mail irradiation process than those packaged in slim-line cases.

Send all three elements in the same envelope or package to:

Library of Congress
Copyright Office
101 Independence Avenue, SE
Washington, DC 20559-****

Use the appropriate four-digit zip code extension to expedite the processing of your claim. In place of ****, use the following:

Literary work: -6222
Visual arts work: -6211
Performing arts work: -6233
Motion picture/AV work: -6238
Sound recording: -6237
Serial issue: -6226

How to use this 2D barcode form

- Complete this form online and then print it out. Do not attempt to print out a blank form. (Form CO is available only online.)
- Print out a second copy for your records. Do not save the form online.
- *Never alter the form by hand after you print it out.* The information you enter is stored in the barcodes on the form. If you submit a hand altered form, you will be charged the higher fee for paper filing.

- If you want to make more than one registration with similar information, keep the form open after you print it; then make the necessary changes and print that version. Repeat as needed. Once you close the form, all the information entered will be lost.
- Both single- and double-sided printing is acceptable.
- *Important printer information:* To achieve best results, use a laser printer. Inkjet printer copies require enlarging if you use the shrink-to-fit-page option. Dot-matrix printer copies are not acceptable.

Line-by-line Instructions   *indicates required fields.   **indicates required alternate fields (one of two required).*

Section 1 - Work Being Registered

1A* *Type of work being registered* · Check the appropriate box. If your work contains more than one type of authorship, choose the type for the predominant authorship in the work.

1B* *Title of work* · Give only one title in this space. To enter an additional title(s), such as titles of individual works in an unpublished collection or works owned by the same claimant in a single unit of publication, click the "additional title" button. Repeat as needed, up to a maximum of 50 titles. (For a registration with more than 50 titles, file electronically or request the appropriate paper application with continuation sheets by mail. See also 1D and 1I below. Give the complete title exactly as it appears on the copy. If there is no title on the copy, give an identifying phrase to serve as the title or state "untitled." Use standard title capitalization without quotation marks; for example, The Old Man and the Sea.

1C *Serial issue* · For serials only, give the required information. **NOTE:** For copyright registration purposes, a serial is a work issued or intended to be issued in successive parts bearing numerical or chronological designations and intended to be continued indefinitely. The classification "serial" includes periodicals, newspapers, magazines, bulletins, newsletters, annuals, journals, proceedings of societies, and other similar works. Enter the ISSN (International Standard Serial Number) without dashes. The Copyright Office does not assign these numbers. For information on obtaining an ISSN, go to *www.loc.gov/issn/*.

1D *Previous or alternative title* · If the work is known by another title, give that title here.

1E* *Year of completion* · Give the year in which creation of *the work you are submitting* was completed. Do not give a year for earlier or later versions. If the work has been published, the year of completion cannot be later than the year of first publication.

1F–1H *Date of publication* · Give the complete date, in mm/dd/yyyy format, on which the work was first published. Do not give a date that is in the future. **NOTE:** Leave this line blank if the work is unpublished. "Publication" is the distribution of copies or phonorecords of a work to the public by sale or other transfer of ownership or by rental, lease, or lending. The offering to distribute copies or phonorecords to a group of persons for purposes of further distribution, public performance, or public display constitutes publication. A public performance or display of a work does not of itself constitute publication. 17 U.S.C. § 101.

1G. *ISBN* · Give the International Standard Book Number (ISBN), if one has been assigned to this work, without dashes. The Copyright Office does not assign these numbers. For information on obtaining an ISBN, contact R.R. Bowker at *www.bowker.com*.

1H *Nation of publication* · Give the nation where the work was first published. Check "United States" in any of the following circumstances: (1) if the work was first published in the United States; (2) if the work was first published simultaneously in the United States and another country; or (3) if the work was first published in another country that is not a "treaty party," and published in the United States within 30 days of first publication. A treaty party is a country other than the United States that is a party to an international copyright agreement. Almost all countries of the world are currently treaty parties. See Circular 38a, *International Copyright Relations of the United States*, for more information. **NOTE:** Leave this line blank if the work is unpublished.

1I *Published as a contribution in a larger work entitled* · If this work has been published as part of a larger work, enter the title of that larger work in this space. Examples of a work published as part of a larger work include a song on a CD, an article in a magazine, and a poem in an anthology. If the larger work includes a volume, number, and/or issue date, add that information on the lines provided.

Section 2 - Author Information

2A** *Personal name* · Complete line 2A or line 2B but not both. The individual who actually created the work is the author except in the case of a "work made for hire," as explained below at 2G. Complete line 2A if the author is an individual. Give the fullest form of the name and skip line 2B.

2B** *Organization name* · Complete line 2A or line 2B but not both. Complete line 2B only if the work is made for hire and a corporation or organization is the author. "Work made for hire" is explained below at 2G. Give the fullest form of the corporate or organizational name.

2C *Doing business as* · You may give the name under which an author does business (doing business as; trading as; sole owner of; also known as).

2D *Year of birth* · Give the year the author was born. The year of birth is optional but is very useful as a form of author identification. Many authors have the same name. **NOTE:** If the year of birth is provided, it will be made part of the online public records produced by the Copyright Office and accessible on the Internet. This information cannot be removed later from those public records.

2E *Year of death* · This information is required if the author is deceased.

2F *Citizenship/domicile* · Check to indicate U.S. citizenship. If the author is a citizen of another country, enter the name of this nation. Alternatively, identify the nation where the author is domiciled (resides permanently).

2G *Author's contribution is* · If this line is applicable, check only one box.

- *Made for hire* · Check this box only if the work was made for hire. This means that:

  1 the work, or an author's contribution to the work, is prepared by an employee as a regular part of his or her employment, or

APPENDIX

2 a work is specially ordered or commissioned in certain instances: for use as a contribution to a collective work, as a part of a motion picture or other audiovisual work, as a translation, as a supplementary work, as a compilation, as an instructional text, as a test, as answer material for a test, or as an atlas, providing the parties agree in writing that the contribution shall be considered a work made for hire. **NOTE:** In this case, name the employer as the author in line 2A or 2B. The employee should not be given. See Circular 9, *Works Made for Hire Under the 1976 Copyright Act*, for more information.

- *Anonymous* · Check this box if no natural person is named as author on copies of the work and the work is not made for hire. In this case, at line 2A, you should either (1) give the author's legal name or (2) state "anonymous" in the "first name" field. Do not leave line 2A blank. If the name is given in line 2A, it will be made part of the online public records produced by the Copyright Office and accessible on the Internet. This information cannot be removed later from those public records.

- *Pseudonymous* · Check this box if the author is identified on copies of the work only under a fictitious name and the work is not made for hire. In this case, check the box and give the pseudonym on the associated line. At line 2A, you should either (1) give the author's legal name or (2) state "pseudonymous" in the "first name" field. Do not leave line 2A blank. If the name is given in line 2A, it will be made part of the online public records produced by the Copyright Office and accessible on the Internet. This information cannot be removed later from those public records.

2H *This author created* · Check the appropriate box(es) that describe this author's contribution to this work. Give a brief statement on the line after "other" only if it is necessary to give a more specific description of the authorship or if none of the check boxes applies. Examples of other authorship statements are choreography, musical arrangement, translation, dramatization, or fictionalization. **NOTE:** Do not give any of the following terms: idea, process, procedure, system, method of operation, concept, principle, discovery, title, or name. These terms refer to elements not subject to copyright. For information on compilations, see the instructions for line 4C.

For a single serial issue, the preferred description of the authorship is usually "collective work." Give this statement at the "other" line. This indicates that the claim is in the collective work as a whole and may include text, editing, compilation, and contribution(s) in which copyright has been transferred to the claimant.

> *For sound recordings and musical works:* Sound recordings and musical works are separate works. To register a claim in both, the copyright claimant(s)/owner(s) must be the same. This requirement generally means the author(s) must be the same. The author of a sound recording is the performer or producer, and the authorship is "sound recording/performance." The author of a musical work—a song, for example—is the composer or song writer and the authorship is "music" or "music and lyrics." See Circular 56A, *Copyright Registration of Musical Compositions and Sound Recordings*, for more information.

Additional authors · To add another author, click the "additional author" button. Repeat as needed.

Section 3 - Copyright Claimant Information

3A✱✱ *Personal name* · Complete line 3A *or* line 3B but not both. Complete line 3A if the claimant is an individual. The copyright claimant (owner) is either the author of the work or the person or organization to whom the copyright has been transferred by an author or other authorized copyright owner. Give the fullest form of the name and skip line 3B.

3B✱✱ *Organization name* · Complete line 3A *or* line 3B but not both. Complete line 3B if the claimant is a corporation or organization. The copyright claimant (owner) is either the author of the work or the person or organization to whom the copyright has been transferred by an author or other authorized copyright owner. Give the fullest form of the corporate or organizational name.

3C *Doing business as* · You may give the name under which a claimant does business (doing business as; trading as; sole owner of; also known as).

3C *Address, email, and phone* · Give this information in the lines provided. **NOTE:** The claimant postal address will be made part of the online public records produced by the Copyright Office and accessible on the Internet. This information cannot be removed later from those public records. The email address and phone number will not appear in the public record unless also included in section 5, Rights and Permissions Contact. Be sure to review section 5 accordingly.

3E *Copyright ownership acquired by* · If the claimant is the author of the work, skip this line. Transfer information is required if this claimant is not an author but has obtained ownership of the copyright from the author or another owner. In this case, check the appropriate box to indicate how ownership was acquired. **NOTE:** "Written agreement" includes a transfer by assignment or by contract. "Will or inheritance" applies only if the person from whom copyright was transferred is deceased. If necessary, check "other" and give a brief statement indicating how copyright was transferred.

Additional claimants · To add another claimant, click the "additional claimant" button. Repeat as needed.

Section 4 - Limitation of Copyright Claim

NOTE: Skip this section unless this work contains or is based on previously registered or previously published material, material in the public domain, or material not owned by this claimant. The purpose of section 4 is to exclude such material from the claim and identify the new material upon which the present claim is based.

4A *Material excluded from this claim* · Check the appropriate box or boxes to exclude any previously registered or previously published material, material in the public domain, or material not owned by this claimant. "Text" may include fiction or nonfiction text, computer program code, lyrics, poetry, or scripts. "Artwork" may include two- or three-dimensional artwork, technical drawings, or photographs. "Audiovisual work" may include video clips, motion picture footage, or a series of images on a CD-ROM. (See the shaded box at the bottom of page 4 for specific examples.) Give a brief statement on the line after "other" only if it is necessary to give a more specific description of the material excluded from this claim or if none of the check boxes applies. **NOTE:** To use someone else's material in your work lawfully, you must have permission from the copyright owner of that material.

4B *Previous registration* · If the work for which you are now seeking registration, or an earlier version of it, has been registered, give the registration number and the year of registration. If there have been multiple registrations, you may give information regarding the last two.

> *Special situation* · If you are registering the first published edition of a work that is identical to a previously registered unpublished version (contains no new material not already registered), check the "other" box in line 4A and state "First publication of work registered as unpublished." In this case, skip line 4C.

4C *New material included in this claim* · Check the appropriate box or boxes to identify the new material you are claiming in this registration. (See the shaded box at the bottom of this paage for specific examples.) Give a brief statement on the line after "other" only if it is necessary to give a more specific description of the new material included in this claim or if none of the check boxes applies. **NOTE:** "Compilation" is a work formed by the collection and assembling of preexisting materials or of data that are selected, coordinated, or arranged in such a way that the resulting work as a whole constitutes an original work of authorship. A claim in "compilation" does not include the material that has been compiled. If that material should also be included in the claim, check the appropriate additional boxes.

Section 5 - Rights and Permissions

This is the person to contact to obtain permission to use this work. If this is the same as the first copyright claimant, simply check the box. **NOTE:** All the information given in section 5, including name, postal address, email address, and phone number, will be made part of the online public records produced by the Copyright Office and accessible on the Internet. This information cannot be removed later from those public records.

Section 6 - Correspondence Contact *

This is the person the Copyright Office should contact with any questions about this application. If this is the same as the first copyright claimant or the rights and permissions contact, simply check the appropriate box. (Information given only in this space will not appear in the online public record.)

Section 7 - Mail Certificate To *

This is the person to whom the registration certificate should be mailed. If this is the same as the first copyright claimant, the rights and permissions contact, or the correspondence contact, simply check the appropriate box. (Information given only in this space will not appear in the online public record.)

Section 8 - Certification

8A● *Handwritten signature* · After you print out the completed application, be sure to sign it at this space.

8B● *Printed name* · Enter the name of the person who will sign the form.

8C● *Date signed* · Choose "today's date" or "write date by hand." In the latter case, be sure to date the application by hand when you sign it. **NOTE:** If this application gives a date of publication, do not certify using a date prior to the publication date.

8D *Deposit account* · Leave this line blank unless you have a Copyright Office deposit account and are charging the filing fee to that account.

8E *Applicant's internal tracking number* · Enter your own internal tracking number, if any.

Section 4 — Examples

Your work	How to complete line 4a (excluded material)	How to complete line 4c (new, additional, or revised material)
New arrangement of a public domain song	Check the "text" and "music" boxes.	State "new arrangement" at the "other" line.
Revised version of a previously published book	Check the "text" box.	Check the "text" box.
English translation of a Spanish novel	Check the "text" box.	State "English translation" at the "other" line.
Movie based on a previously registered screenplay	Check the "text" box.	State "All other cinematographic material" at the "other" line.

U.S. Copyright Office · Library of Congress · 101 Independence Avenue SE · Washington, DC 20559-6000 · www.copyright.gov

FORM CO   REV: 08/2009

Inventors' Organizations by State

Organization	Address	Phone	Website/E-mail
National			
United Inventors Association of the USA	999 Lehigh Station Road Henrietta, NY 14467-9311	1-800-701-8595	Web: *www.uiausa.org* E-mail: *admin@uiausa.org*
Alabama			
Invent Alabama	137 Mission Circle Montevallo, AL 35115	(205) 663-9982	
Alaska			
Alaska Inventors & Entrepreneurs	P.O. Box 241801 Anchorage, AK 99524-1801	(907) 563-4337	E-mail: *inventor@arctic.net*
Inventors Institute of Alaska	P.O. Box 876154 Wasilla, AK 99687	(907) 376-5114	
Arkansas			
Inventors Congress Inc.	Rt. 2 Box 1630 Dandanell, AR 72834	(501) 229-4515	
Arizona			
Inventors Association of Arizona	P.O. Box 6436 Glendale, AZ 85312	(570) 721-8540	Web: *www.azinventors.org* E-mail: *exdir@azinventors.org*
California			
Inventors Forum	P.O. Box 1008 Huntington Beach, CA 92647-1008	(714) 540-2491	Web: *www.inventorsforum.org* E-mail: *info@inventorsforum.org*
Inventors Alliance	P.O. Box 390219 Mountain View, CA 94039-390219	(650) 964-1576 or (877) 468-3689	Web: *www.inventorsalliance.org* E-mail: *president@inventorsalliance.org*
Central Valley Inventors' Association	P.O. Box 1551 Manteca, CA 95336	(209) 239-5414	E-mail: *cdesigns@softcom.net*

Organization	Address	Phone	Website/E-mail
California cont'd			
Contra Costa Inventors Club	295 Stevenson Drive Pleasant Hill, CA 94523-4149		
San Diego Inventors Group	11190 Poblado Road San Diego, CA 92127	(858) 673-4733	
Bruce Sawyer Center	606 Heelburg Santa Rosa, CA 95401	(707) 524-1773	
American Inventor Network	1320 High School Road Sebastopol, CA 95472	(707) 823-3865	
Inventors Forum chapter in Whittier	14034 Oval Drive Whittier, CA 90605	(562) 464-0069	Web: **www.inventorsforum.org** E-mail: **info@inventorsforum.org** or **AnthonyH@inventorsforum.org**
Colorado			
Rocky Mountain Inventors Association	1805 S. Bellaire St., Ste. 480 Denver, CO 80222	(303) 831-4133	Web: **www.rminventor.org**
Connecticut			
Inventors Association of Connecticut	521 Popes Island Road Milford, CT 06461	(203) 924-9538	Web: **www.inventus.org** E-mail: **lyon@docjava.com**
D.C.			
Inventors Network of the Capital Area	P.O. Box 18052 Baltimore, MD 21220	(443) 794- 7350	E-mail: **ipatent@aol.com**
Delaware			
Delaware Entrepreneurs Forum	P.O. Box 278 Yorklyn, DE 19736	(302) 234-4440	
Florida			
Edison Inventors Association Inc.	P.O. Box 07398 Fort Myers, FL 33919	(941) 275-4332	E-mail: **drghn@aol.com**

Organization	Address	Phone	Website/E-mail
Florida cont'd			
Tampa Bay Inventors Council	5901 Third St. South St. Petersburg, FL 33705-5305	(727) 565-2085	Web: *http://tbic.us* E-mail: *admin@tbic.us*
Inventors Council of Central Florida	4855 Big Oaks Lane Orlando, FL 32806-7826	(407) 859-4855	
Space Coast Inventors Guild	1221 Pine Tree Drive Indian Harbour Beach, FL 32937	(407) 773-4031	
Georgia			
Inventor Associates of Georgia Inc.	3356 Station Court Lawrenceville, GA 30044-5674		E-mail: *rreardon@bellsouth.net*
Iowa			
Drake University Inventure Program	SBDC-Drake University 2507 University Ave. Des Moines, IA 50311	(515) 271-2655	
Idaho			
East Idaho Inventors Forum	P.O. Box 452 Shelly, ID 83274	(208) 346-6763	E-mail: *wordinjj@ida.net*
Illinois			
Inventors' Council	431 S. Dearborne #705 Chicago, IL 60605	(312) 939-3329	E-mail: *patent@donmoyer.com*
Illinois Innovators & Inventor's Club	P.O. Box 623 Edwardsville, IL 62025	(618) 656-7445	E-mail: *invent@charter-il.com*
Indiana			
Indiana Inventors Association	5514 S. Adams Marion, IN 46953	(765) 674-2845	E-mail: *arhumbert@busprod.com*

Organization	Address	Phone	Website/E-mail
Kansas			
Inventors Association of South-Central Kansas	2302 N. Amarado St. Wichita, KS 67205	(316) 721-1866	Web: *http://inventkansas.com* E-mail: *inventor@inventkansas.com*
Mid-America Inventors Association	P.O. Box 2678 Kansas City, KS 66110	(913) 495-9465	Web: *www.midamerica-inventors.com* E-mail: *midamerica-inventors@kc.rr.com*
Kentucky			
Central Kentucky Inventors & Entrepreneurs	117 Carolyn Drive Nicholasville, KY 40356	(606) 885-9593	E-mail: *nashky@IBM.net*
Louisiana			
Louisiana Inventors Association	14724 Vinewood Drive, Baton Rouge, LA 70815	(225) 752-3783	*info@recyclerecycle.com*
Maine			
Portland Inventors Forum	Dept Industrial Co-op University of Maine 5717 Corbett Hall Orono, ME 04469-5717	(207) 581-1488	E-mail: *jsward@maine.edu*
Maryland			
Invention Resource International	10 South Street, Baltimore, MD 21202	(410) 962-1122	
Massachusetts			
Inventors Association of New England	P.O. Box 335 Lexington, MA 02420-0004	(781) 274-8500	Web: *www.inventne.org* E-mail: *rhausslein@rcn.com*
Worcester Area Inventors	132 Sterling St. West Boylston, MA 01583	(508) 835-6435	E-mail: *barbara@nedcorp.com*
Innovators' Resource Network	Pelham West Associates P.O. Box 137 Shutesbury, MA 01072		Web: *www.irnetwork.org* E-mail: *info@irnetwork.org*

Organization	Address	Phone	Website/E-mail
Michigan			
Inventors Clubs of America	524 Curtis Road East Lansing, MI 48823	(517) 332-3561	
Inventors Council of Mid-Michigan	P.O. Box 232 Lennon, MI 48449-0232	(810) 245-5599	Web: *http://inventorscouncil.org* E-mail: *icmm@inventorscouncil.org*
Inventors Club of Michigan	24685 Ravine Circle, Apt. 203 Farmington Hills, MI 48335	(810) 870-9139	
Minnesota			
Minnesota Inventors Congress	235 S. Mill St. P.O. Box 71 Redwood Falls, MN 56283	(507) 627-2344 or (800) 468-3681	Web: *www.inventhelper.org* E-mail: *info@ minnesotainventorscongress.org*
Society of Minnesota Inventors	P.O. Box 252 St. Francis, MN 55070	(763) 753-2766	E-mail: *paulparis@uswest.net*
Inventors' Network	23 Empire Drive, Ste. 105 St. Paul, MN 55103	(612) 602-3175	
Missouri			
Mid-America Inventors Association	8911 E. 29th St. Kansas City, MO 64129-1502	(816) 254-9542	
Inventors Association of St. Louis	P.O. Box 410111 St. Louis, MO 63141	(314) 432-1291	
Mississippi			
Society of Mississippi Inventors	3825 Ridgewood Road Jackson, MS 39211	(662) 915-5001	
Montana			
Yellowstone Inventors	3 Carrie Lynn Billings, MT 59102	(406) 259-9110	

Organization	Address	Phone	Website/E-mail
Montana Inventors Association	5350 Love Lane Bozeman, MT 59178	(406) 586-1541	
North Dakota			
Northern Plains Inventors Congress	2534 S. University Drive, Ste. 4 Fargo, ND 58103	(701) 281-8822 or (800) 281-7009	Web: *www.ndinventors.com* E-mail: *info@neustel.com*
Lincoln Inventors Association	92 Ideal Way Brainard, NE 68626	(402) 545-2179	
Nevada			
Nevada Inventors Association	P.O. Box 11008 Reno, NV 89510-1008	(775) 677-4824	Web: *www.nevadainventors.org* E-mail: *rvrdl@aol.com* or *costar@ibm.net*
Inventors Society of Southern Nevada	3627 Huerta Drive Las Vegas, NV 89121	(702) 435-7741	E-mail: *inventssn@aol.com*
New Hampshire			
New Hampshire Inventors Association	P.O. Box 2772 Concord, NH 03302-2772	(603) 228-3854	E-mail: *john@nhinventor.com*
New Jersey			
Jersey Shore Inventors Club	416 Park Place Ave. Bradley Beach, NJ 07720	(732) 776-8467	E-mail: *2edeilmcclain@msn.com*
National Society of Inventors	94 N. Rockledge Drive Livingston, NJ 07039-1121	(973) 994-9282	
New Jersey Entrepreneurs Forum	P.O. Box 313 Westfield, NJ 07090	(908) 789-3424	
New Mexico			
New Mexico Inventors Club	P.O. Box 30062 Albuquerque, NM 87190	(505) 266-3541	

Organization	Address	Phone	Website/E-mail
New York			
Inventors Alliance of America-Buffalo Chapter	300 Pearl St. Olympic Towers, Ste. 200 Buffalo, NY 14202	(716) 842-4561	E-mail: *ellwood@netcom.ca*
NY Society of Professional Inventors	Box 216 Farmingdale, NY 11735-9996	(516) 798-1490	
Inventors Alliance of America – Rochester Chapter	97 Pinebrook Drive Rochester, NY 14616	(716) 225-3750	E-mail: *InventNY@aol.com*
Ohio			
Inventors Network of Greater Akron	1741 Stone Creek Lane Twinsburg, OH 44087	(330) 425-1749	
Inventors' Council of Cincinnati	3178 Victoria Ave. Cincinnati, OH 45208	(513) 321-7280 or (513) 772-9333	
Inventors Connection Greater Cleveland	P.O. Box 360804 Cleveland, OH 44136	(216) 226-9681	E-mail: *icgc@usa.com*
Innovation Alliance	2000 Henderson Road, #140 Columbus, OH 43220	(614) 326-3822	
Inventors Network Inc.	1275 Kinnear Road Columbus, OH 43212	(614) 470-0144	E-mail: *13832667@msn.com*
Inventors Council of Canton	303 55th St. NW North Canton, OH 44720	(330) 499-1262	
Inventors Council of Dayton	P.O. Box 611 Dayton, OH 45409-0611	(937) 293-2770	E-mail: *geopierce@earthlink.net*
Inventors Council of Greater Lorain	1101 Park Ave. Elyria, OH 44035	(216) 322-1540	

Organization	Address	Phone	Website/E-mail
Ohio cont'd			
Youngstown-Warren Inventors' Association.	500 City Center One P.O. Box 507 Youngstown, OH 44501-0507	(330) 744-4481	E-mail: *mm@cisnet.com*
Oklahoma			
Oklahoma Inventors Congress	3212 NW 35th St. Oklahoma City, OK 73112	(405) 947-5782	E-mail: *wbaker@tanet.net*
Oregon			
South Oregon Inventors Council	332 W. Sixth St.- Medford, OR 97501	(541) 772-3478	E-mail: *SBDC@ S. Oregon State*
Pennsylvania			
American Society of Inventors	P.O. Box 58426 Philadelphia, PA 19102	(215) 546-6601	Web: *www.americaninventor.org* E-mail: *info@asoi.org*
Pennsylvania Inventors Association	2317 E. 43rd St. Erie, PA 16510	(814) 825-5820	E-mail: *jgorniak@pa-invent.org*
Northwest Inventors Council	Gannon University Erie, PA 16541	(814) 871-7619	
Inventors Council – Pittsburgh	110 Rock Run Road Elizabeth, PA 15037	(412) 751-6545	
South Carolina			
Carolina Inventors Council	2960 Dacusville Highway Easley, SC 29640	(864) 859-0066	E-mail: *john17@home.com*
Tennessee			
Tennessee Inventors Association	P.O. Box 11225 Knoxville, TN 37939-1225	(865) 483-0151	Web: *www.uscni.com/tia*

Organization	Address	Phone	Website/E-mail
Texas			
Houston Inventors Association	2916 W. T.C. Jester Blvd., Ste. 100 Houston, TX 77018	(713) 686-7676	Web: **www.inventors.org/index.htm** E-mail: **kenroddy@nol.net**
Laredo Inventors Association	210 Palm Circle Laredo, TX 78041	(956) 725-5863	
Network of American Inventors & Entrepreneurs	P.O. Box 667113 Houston, TX 77006	(713) 523-3923	E-mail: **info@naie.org**
Texas Inventors Association	2912 Trophy Drive Plano, TX 75025	(972) 312-0090	E-mail: **wisepatents@sbcglobal.net**
Vermont			
Inventors Network of Vermont	4 Park St. Springfield, VT 05156	(802) 885-8178 or (802) 885-5100	E-mail: **comtu@turbont.net**
Virginia			
Inventors Network of the Capital Area	P.O. Box 15150 Arlington, VA 22202	(703) 971-9216	E-mail: **info@inca.hispeed.com**
Association for Science, Technology & Innovation	Box 1242 Arlington, VA 22210	(703) 241-2850	
Blue Ridge Inventors' Club	P.O. Box 7451 Charlottesville, VA 22906-7451	(804) 973-0276 or (804) 973-3708	Web: **http://blueridgeinventorsclub.org** E-mail: **info@blueridgeinventorsclub.org**
Washington			
Northwest Inventors Guild	P.O. Box 226 Port Hadlock, WA 98339	(360) 821-5919 or (360) 385-6863	E-mail: **aero1@waypt.com**
Whidbey Island Inventor Network	P.O. Box 1026 Langley, WA 98260	(360) 321-4447	E-mail: **wiin@whidbey.com**
Inventors Network	P.O. Box 5575 Vancouver, WA 98668	(503) 239-8299	

Organization	Address	Phone	Website/E-mail
Washington			
Tri-Cities Enterprise Assn.	2000 Logston Blvd. Richland, WA 99352	(509) 375-3268	
Wisconsin			
Wisconsin Innovation Service Center	1200 Hyland Hall, University of Wisconsin-Whitewater Whitewater, WI 53190	(262) 472-1365	

SOURCE: NATIONAL INVENTOR FRAUD CENTER

Invention Checklist

Below is a list of the key points along your journey of inventing. Your personal journey might involve a variation of this list, as you may skip certain steps in favor of other things.

The Idea

❏ Create Inventor's Notebook

❏ Describe Your Idea/Invention

❏ Sketch Your Invention in the Inventor's Notebook

Intellectual Property

❏ Conduct a Patent Search

❏ Meet with a Patent Attorney

❏ File Patent and/or other Intellectual Property Protection

Market Research

❏ Identify the Market for your Invention

❏ Identify the Major Competitors in the Market

Design

❏ Create Sketches of the Invention (revise as necessary)

❏ Design Invention Using CAD

❏ Create a Model or Have It Created

❏ Make Revisions/Changes to Model

❏ Create Prototype or Have It Created

❏ Make Revisions/Changes to Prototype

Commercialization/Manufacturing

❏ Obtain Financing

❏ Research Manufacturers and/or Licensees

❑ Decide What Commercialization Route is Best for You (e.g., Sell Idea, License

License Idea or Manufacture Yourself

If You Maintain Control of Your Idea:
❑ Find Manufacturer
❑ Develop Packaging
❑ Create Marketing Plan
❑ Publish Website
❑ Plan Distribution Channels

If You License Your Idea
❑ Find Potential Licensees
❑ Contact Licensees/Set Up Meetings
❑ Create Presentation
❑ Decide on a Licensee
❑ Negotiate Contract

Bibliography

Bird, Pamela Riddle, PhD. *Inventing for Dummies*. Hoboken, NJ: Wiley Publishing. 2004.

Charmasson, Henri. *Patents, Copyrights and Trademarks for Dummies*. Hoboken, NJ: Wiley Publishing. 2004.

Churchill, Gilbert A., Jr. and Peter, J. Paul. *Marketing: Creating Value for Customers*. NY, NY: McGraw-Hill. 1998.

Department of Defense. "The DoD SBIR & STTR Programs." **www.acq.osd.mil/osbp/sbir.**

Docie, Ronald Louis, Sr. *The Inventor's Bible*. Berkeley, CA: Ten Speed Press. 2004.

Gahl, Derek. "How to Harness the Marketing Power of Blogs." Entrepeneur.com. March 2006. **www.entrepreneur.com/ebusiness/ ebusinesscolumnist/article84232.html.**

Harvard University Office of Technology Development. *Inventor's Handbook.* 2009. **www.techtransfer.harvard.edu/resources/guidelines/ inventorhandbook/Inventor-Handbook.pdf.**

Hawkins, Del I., Best, Roger J., and Coney, Kenneth A. *Consumer Behavior: Building Marketing Strategy.* NY, NY: McGraw-Hill. 2001.

Kiraly, Suzanne. North American Product Certification Marks and the Testing and Certification Process. CSA International: **www.csa-international.org/media/whitepapers/pdfs/ NorthAmericanCertificationMarks&theTesting&Cert.Process.pdf.** See also **www.csa-international.org/about.**

Kitchen Cabinet Manufacturers Association. **www.kcma.org.**

Kracke, Don. *Turn Your Idea or Invention into Millions.* NY, NY: Allworth Press. 2001.

Lander, Jack. "Should You License or Manufacture Your Invention? Here's what to consider when deciding whether to license your invention or manufacture it yourself." Nolo. **www.nolo.com/legal-encyclopedia/ article-29775.html.**

Levy, Richard. *The Complete Idiot's Guide to Cashing in on Your Inventions.* NY, NY: Alpha Books/Penguin Press. 2002.

Meerman Scott, David. *The New Rules of Marketing & PR: How to Use News Releases, Blogs, Podcasting, Viral Marketing & Online Media to Reach Buyers Directly.* Hoboken, NJ: Wiley Publishing. 2007.

National Inventor Fraud Center: **www.inventorfraud.com/ inventorgroups.htm.**

Pressman, David. *Patent It Yourself.* Berkeley, CA: Nolo. 1985.

Reese, Harvey. *How to License Your Million Dollar Idea: Everything You Need to Know to Turn a Simple Idea into a Million Dollar Payday.* NY, NY: Wiley Publishing. 2002.

Riddle Bird, Pamela. *Inventing for Dummies.* Hoboken, NJ: Wiley Publishing. 2004.

Ries, Al and Trout, Jack. *Positioning: The Battle for Your Mind.* NY, NY: McGraw-Hill. 2001.

Safco, Lon & Brake, David. *The Social Media Bible: Tactics, Tools, and Strategies for Business Success.* Hoboken, NJ: Wiley Publishing. 2009.

Schoenherr, Steven E., Professor (retired) of history at the University of San Diego. "The history of the computer." **http://history.sandiego.edu/ GEN/recording/computer1.html.**

Singh, Shiv. *Social Media Marketing for Dummies*. Hoboken, NJ: Wiley Publishing. 2010.

Tozzi, John. "How to Sell Your Invention." Bloomberg Businessweek. September 2007. **www.businessweek.com/smallbiz/content/sep2007/sb20070912_726423.htm**.

U.S. Patent and Trademark Office: **www.USPTO.gov**.

Zimmer, Ed, and Westrum, Ron. "The Inventors' Study Project - a Progress Report." Inventors' Network of the Capital Area. Volume 9, Issue 3. March 2007. **www.dcinventors.org/newsletters/2001_March_Inventors_Network_of_the_Capital_Area_Newsletter.pdf**.

About the Author

Janessa Castle has been a writer and an editor for the past ten years and has worked with numerous businesses and individuals on various projects. She has worked with a variety of clients including published and aspiring authors, company executives, public relations and marketing departments, politicians, and publishing companies.

Janessa was a journalism instructor at Ohio State University. She taught writing and copy editing to journalism and strategic communications students for six years. She also was the adviser of *The Lantern*, Ohio State's student newspaper, in the summers for four years.

Janessa has a master's degree in communications from Ohio State University and completed two years of full-time course work for her doctorate in the same program. She has a bachelor's degree in public relations from Capital University.

Index

T

U

V

W